BRA

Martin Sloboda (1974) was born into an old
Bratislava family and lives in Bratislava. He followed
courses in English and German studies; while a
student, he also worked as a tourist guide. After
graduation he established MS AGENCY, s.r.o. which
acts as a publisher of tourist literature and a guiding
and events agency. He is the author of several
successful guides as well as being a photographer
- most of the pictures in his books are his own. He
accompanies top-level state visits and diplomats
in Bratislava and gives lectures about Slovakia. Let
yourself be guided by a professional who will inspire
you with his sense of detail and love for his native
town.

MARTIN (••) SLOBODA

How to Use This Book

1 Organisation of the Book

This book has ten main chapters. Each chapter is distinguished by a different coloured strip at the edges of the pages. The table above shows the colours by which the individual chapters are distinguished. Each chapter begins with an introductory double-page with the contents of the chapter. It contains sub-chapters usually spreading over a double-page. Each sub-chapter has five to ten points. Each point refers to a paragraph with a numbered heading. It describes a particular place, event, topic etc. The points chosen include pictures and maps and they are numbered according to the heading of the point. Some chapters contain small maps or ground-plans with numbered sites where an object or

a heritage site are located. Or the map may depict a route for sightseeing. The numbering of

Box containing suggestion or an event/place of interest 😯 / 🛐

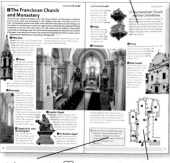

Information box ⓘ   Ground-plan

the pictures relates only to a page/double-page of a sub-chapter, respectively. There is no connection between the numbering of the individual sub-chapters. At the ends of the paragraphs of the points, links to web-pages are given in tables by means of 🌐 (www) or other contact data, telephone and fax numbers 📞, e-mail @. If a location described is shown in a map in the book, its coordinates are given with a symbol 🗺 at the end of a paragraph.

A chapter may contain individual frames with symbols 😯 or 🛐. The symbol 😯 indicates an historical event of interest related to a particular location and the symbol 🛐 indicates a suggestion for a visit or an important event. The chapter Walks & Trips includes information tables for each sub-chapter. In the information tables, information is given for a particular locality such as: distance from Bratislava; time required to reach a particular place; means of transport; recommended sites to visit; contacts, etc.

🗺 3 AB 12

Map number | Horizontal coordinate | Vertical coordinate

Sub-chapter   Sub-chapter point

Traditional Dishes

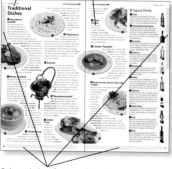

Coloured identification of chapters

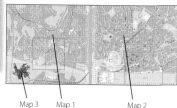

Map 3   Map 1   Map 2

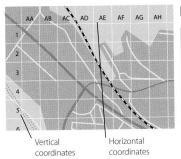

Vertical coordinates   Horizontal coordinates

2 Using a Map

Each map has a net of coordinates to aid in locating a particular place on the map. It is indicated with a symbol 🔍 followed by 4 – 5 digit coordinates. They consist of the following figures: Map number; horizontal position; vertical position

The maps are to be found within the book and on the inside covers and each one is numbered. The horizontal coordinates are identified by means of a pair of letters; their combinations are unique to each map in order to avoid any confusion. The numbering of the vertical coordinates is the same for each map. In order to make orientation around the map easier, the identification of the grids of coordinates is provided on all the maps. To find a particular place on the map, first find the particular map on the page on the inside cover. Then, find its horizontal and vertical coordinates identified by letters and numbers. The whole map is covered with a network of white lines to help you search the locality. The location you want is where the horizontal and vertical coordinates intersect. The key to all three maps inside the cover is on Map 2. Explanations for other symbols used in the maps are in the next column.

3 Contents, Indices and Orientation in the Book

The contents of the book are shown inside the front cover. It contains chapters and sub-chapters. The third level – the sub-chapter points - are on the introductory double-page of each chapter. The final chapter is a general index and a street index. The general index comprises a selection of the most important words with the pages where they can be found. The street index contains a list of all streets and their coordinates on Map 2. If a street or feature extends across several grid-squares, it is identified by the coordinates corresponding to its approximate centre.

4 Key to symbols

🛣	length of route
📍	distance from Bratislava - centre
🚶	pedestrian walkway
🛼	walkway for in-line skaters
🚲	cycle path
🚗	car
🚃	train
🚌	bus
🚠	cable-lift
🕐🚶	time by foot
🕐🛼	time by in-line skates
🕐🚲	time by bike
🕐🚗	time by car
🕐🚃	time by train
🕐🚌	time by bus
🏰	castle
🔍	reference to a map in the book
🖱	internet address on www
ℹ	information
📞	telephone
@	email
📖	historical event of interest
☝	recommendation
🍴	restaurant
🍷	wine/beer tasting
🛏	accommodation
🎁	souvenirs/handmade products

Welcome

1 Unique Location

Whoever in the past decided that there would be a town in this place laid down the foundation for its later prosperity. Except when trade and development have been impeded by wars, regimes and borders, Bratislava has always been a flourishing and prosperous town which has made the most of its strategic position on the Danube and at the intersections of important European trade routes. In the Mediaeval period and later in the 18th century, Bratislava was a significant economic centre and later also a cultural and political centre of Central Europe.

It was thanks to its location that Bratislava in the 16th century became the capital and coronation town of the Hungarian Kingdom and the place where its crown jewels were kept. For one thing, it was remote from the invading Turks, but on the other hand it was conveniently close to imperial Vienna, from where the whole of the Austro-Hungarian Empire was to be governed for the following almost 500 years. Vienna and Bratislava were very closely connected economically, culturally and politically, for a long time. In the 18th century the Castle was rebuilt and served as a summer residence for Queen Maria Theresa who visited the town frequently due to its proximity to Vienna. Another reason for her frequent visits was the fact that her favourite daughter Maria Christine lived here for almost 20 years.

What had in the past been a long-term advantage, suddenly in the middle of the 20th century came to constitute a major disadvantage and Bratislava was obliged to pay heavily for its unique position. After the communists came to power in 1948, an Iron Curtain, visible from the city centre, was drawn which brutally divided what had been a single economic and cultural region. Following the fall of commusim in 1989, Bratislava could at last develop as a free town and re-establish close relations with Vienna. Now, paradoxically, it was Vienna which held the excluded region back from its more rapid growth. Although much was resolved once Slovakia became a member of the European Union in 2004, the final impediment to the rapid development of the cross-border Euro-region was removed as late as 2007 when a motorway on the Austrian side came into operation and Slovakia became part of the Schengen group.

2 Multi-Cultural Past

Like many other towns in the former Austro-Hungarian Empire, the co-existence of various ethnic groups and the mixture of different languages and cultures were also typical features of Bratislava. From its foundation in the 13th century up to the second half of the 19th century, Bratislava was dominated by German-speaking citizens. This, however, does not mean that the city was exclusively German. Already in the Mediaeval period, Italians, Slovaks and Hungarians lived here, a significant community of Jews settled in the city, and later Croatians, Bulgarians and finally Czechs came to live here. It was a mix of ethnic groups and religions, a sort of well-stirred and spiced "goulash" that the citizens were rightly proud of. Nevertheless, the situation should not be idealised, and undoubtedly there were problems when one group sought to gain more privileges at the expense of others. But it always stayed within civilised limits. Each ethnic group specialised in different activities; they needed to work together with the others and they complemented each other. The Germans were craftsmen, traders and wine producers, the Hungarians were aristocrats and clerks, the Slovaks market traders and housekeepers, the Bulgarians grew vegetables and the Jews were traders, etc. This was the source of the wealth of old Bratislava, a town which each group called by its own name: It was Pressburg in German, Pozsony in Hungarian, up to 1919 Prešporok in Slovak then Bratislava. Many citizens were able to speak three languages although there were only a few who were capable of conversing in all three languages at a higher level. Mixing all three languages together in the local dialect was the more usual state of affairs. An inhabitant of the city was first of all a Pressburger and only after that a member of a particular national group. Following World War I, a large number of Slovaks and Czech state administrative workers moved into the city so the ratios of the ethnic groups were balanced. Between the wars the city was officially trilingual (Slovak, German and Hungarian); signs on shops were written in three languages and shop assistants welcomed customers to a shop in three languages.

3 Human Catastrophe

At the end of the nineteen-thirties, multi-cultural Bratislava did not remain immune to the spreading German Nazi propaganda and sections of the German and Slovak populations became radicalised. The balance was disturbed and, all of a sudden, what divided people became more important than what had joined them together for centuries. The first to experience the altered balance was the Jewish community. Most of the Jews (then 10% of the inhabitants of Bratislava) were deported to Auschwitz and they never returned. Before World War II, almost 30% of the inhabitants were German speakers and 20 % Hungarians. After the war, most of the German- and some of the Hungarian-speaking inhabitants were deported from the republic on the basis of "collective guilt".

Following the regime change in 1948, the communists' aim was not only to make Bratislava Slovak, which meant eliminating all the other nationalities based in Bratislava, but also to eradicate the middle class (including Slovak). In forced re-settlement upheavals, the middle class and non-communist intelligentsia were forced to move from Bratislava and were spread over the whole of Slovakia and the proletariat from all over Slovakia moved to Bratislava. The confiscated properties were given to people with a demonstrable proletarian background who were actively involved in the Communist Party. This social, cultural and subsequently architectural destruction of Bratislava was augmented by a massive migration due to the expansion of industry and administration. Only later, from the sixties on, did natural migration dominate when young people came to Bratislava to gain their higher education and, following graduation, they stayed on in the city. All of these people needed cheap and readily available accommodation. In the space of forty years, the number of inhabitants increased three-fold and the city came to be surrounded by extensive concrete blocks of flats. The city was governed by people who bore no relation to the city, its history and traditions, and who gave the go-ahead to the steady devastation of the Old Town and, in the name of "progress", the demolition of extensive quarters below the Castle. When the "Iron Curtain" was lifted in 1989, Bratislava presented only a sad picture of a bleak, grey, provincial industrial town with neglected infrastructure. The war itself was not the cause of the physical destruction of the city, as was the case in many other European cities. It was the two brutal regimes which caused and resulted from the war and which destroyed the 700-year old co-existence and mutual enrichment of various ethnic groups and cultures. Even more remarkable, then, was the restoration of the city and its relation with its past which followed.

4 Capital

Following the division of Czechoslovakia in 1993, Bratislava became the capital of the Slovak Republic. As the second largest city of the former Czechoslovakia (450,000 inhabitants), it stepped out from under the shadow of Prague and began to develop as the capital of the independent state. Along with the change of regime, this meant investments into the city from private and state sources. The citizens readily identified with the new role of Bratislava as the capital and also with its multi-cultural

past, which formerly had been perceived rather negatively. Although most of the current inhabitants are migrants who came to the city after World War II in search of jobs and to acquire an education, the city managed to successfully "infect" them with its genius loci. The new generation that was born here and that is currently gradually becoming the leader of the city comprises confident and proud Bratislavans. Despite all the destruction in the 20th century, enough of the "Pressburg spirit" has been retained to continue the positive message of the old Bratislava. In comparison with other European cities, the average age of Bratislavans is relatively low and the educational level of the city is high. In Bratislava there are a large number of universities and the overall number of students reaches 65,000. At the end of the nineties, a complex restoration of the Old Town was set in motion and today it shines as it did in the past and evokes the atmosphere of the old Bratislava. The city attracts more and more visitors and also foreigners who come to live and work here. Gradually, Bratislava is taking on its cosmopolitan character although under completely different conditions. Where German was recently widespread, its place today has been taken by English.

5 Economic Boom

The city once again profits enormously from its strategic position at a time when borders connect rather than divide. Following 1989, the positive aspects of economic transformation of the country affected Bratislava first. The chemical industry in the city has been transformed and the city's economy is directed towards more sophisticated production and services. Despite a strong industrial background, it is services which produce two-thirds of the city's GDP. The biggest enterprise in the city, as well as in Slovakia as a whole, is Volkswagen which has in Bratislava a factory producing luxury SUVs. The accelerated development of the city started at the turn of millennium and in

📜 Historical Overview

100 BC
Biatec

Celtic oppidum

AD 300-400
Roman station Gerulata in today's Rusovce

864 Dowina
First written record of Devín Castle in the annals of Fulda

907 Brezalauspurch
First written record of the town in the annals of Salzburg

Around 1000
Stephen I, founder of the kingdom of Hungary

1241 - 1242
Invasion and devastation by hordes of Tatars

1291
King Andrew III grants the town municipal priviliges

1436
King Sigismund of Luxembourg grants the town its coat-of-arms

1465
King Matthias Corvinus founds Universitas Istropolitana - the first university on the territory of present-day Slovakia

1526
After the Battle of Mohács large parts of Hungary fall under Ottoman rule

the past few years Bratislava has experienced an unprecedented boom in all areas of development which is very evident. The Danube has become a new site for development; a massive building activity is taking place along its banks which will not only add attractive new quarters by the river to the city centre but it will also give Bratislava a metropolitan character.

One of Bratislava's advantages is its young and educated population whose number substantially exceeds the number in the neighbouring capitals. Due to this advantage, in recent years the city has become directed towards research and development of technologies, pure production with high added value and services. Unemployment reaches 3% while Bratislava Region is ranked 5th by Eurostat in terms of purchasing power parity in the EU. Both capitals see their future in even closer collaboration and reducing distances also with the help of the Twin City project. Today, there are no remaining obstacles to hold back the heart of central Europe from its natural development as one of the most dynamically developing regions in Europe. Vienna-Bratislava in 45 minutes by car was still regarded as science fiction some years ago. Today, however, it is an everyday reality.

6 City of Contrasts

Bratislava gives the impression of being a city of great urban and architectural contrasts. This is associated with several waves of abrupt development which have taken place in the city. Up to the 18th century, the town developed relatively steadily. In the 18th century, the first more extensive building boom resulted from developments in the economy and the presence of the royal family. As a consequence, Hungarian aristocrats commissioned the building of their palaces which are still to be seen in the city. The return of the capital to Budapest at the end of the 18th century resulted in a long-term stagnation of the town which was interrupted by the development of industry in the second half of the 19th century. Due to this stagnation, Bratislava did not experience its "belle époque" with broad boulevards and elegant streets to such an extent as other big towns in the region. The situation changed in the inter-war period when a young generation of architects tried to bring to a close the era of over-decorated forms and introduce progressive, modern architecture. As a result, in the twenties and thirties, some remarkable works were created which were several decades ahead of their time. Many of the modern-looking buildings in the city centre originate from this period.

The era which had the most pronounced impact on the appearance of Bratislava started in the sixties when pre-fabricated concrete panel technology was applied, resulting in the massive building of concrete blocks of flats. Due to this unified technology, it was possible to construct extensive blocks of flats in a relatively short time and cheaply. The price paid for it was a low standard of building and underdeveloped infrastructure. In recent years, Bratislava has been experiencing the greatest building boom to date which has substantially changed the appearance of the city. Now it is banks, business and shopping centres and residential towers. Symbolic of this stage of development are the numerous sky-scrapers which are being erected all over the city. There is no other city in the whole of Central Europe with as many different faces as Bratislava within a relatively small space.

7 High Culture

As early as the 18th century, Bratislava was noted for its rich cultural and musical life. Due to the presence of members of the royal family and aristocracy, the town was frequently visited by a number of famous artists. Families of aristocrats kept pianists as music teachers for their children. Mozart and Beethoven gave their concerts in this town, Haydn and Liszt were frequent visitors here, Marschner and Rubinstein worked here,

Hummel, Dohnányi and Schmidt were born in this town and Bartók studied here. Plays and operas were performed at first in the palaces of aristocrats and, from 1776, in the town's theatre. Haydn himself came here to introduce his operas; here his masses were conducted by none other than Liszt himself. In the period between the wars renowned artists such as Max Reinhardt, Oskar Nedbal, Richard Strauss, Pietro Mascagni or Emmy Destinn gave their performances here in theatres and operas. The centuries of intensive cultural life have left a deep impression which can be sensed merely in the course of a stroll through the Old Town. The communist regime supported culture selectively, especially classical music and opera which were to serve as a "shop-window" in the West. From its unbroken tradition, in the second half of the 20th century, Slovakia gave the world a number of famous musicians and opera singers. That is why anyone who is keen on this kind of music should not miss the opportunity to go to the opera or philharmonic. This strong musical tradition is reflected in many musical festivals of various genres from classical music to jazz. There is also a long tradition in balls which, during the season, are organised in their tens if not hundreds. Although Bratislava does not possess world-famous museums and galleries full of works of reputable masters, its centre is dotted with various smaller even miniature museums and galleries which promise no less of an original experience.

8 Young Spirit

Although the Old Town is not extensive, the concentration of historical sites, galleries, museums as well as cafés, restaurants and bars is so great as to cause you just to wonder. The whole of the Old Town forms a pedestrian zone which is transformed into one large terrace in summer. The Old Town lives its rich life every day, not only on week-ends, and a sense of joie de vivre and joy spreads over everywhere. You will probably get a sense of it being more like a seaside town than a town in Central Europe. You will also have the feeling that the is relatively low.

It is one thing to reconstruct the whole of the Old Town but it is quite another to breathe life into it as has happened in Bratislava. It was only relatively recently that the Old Town was quite literally dilapidated and dead. This radical change deserves high praise. Various activities persuaded Bratislavans to go strolling, entertaining or just relaxing in the Old Town. It has not taken a long time and no attraction and persuasion have been necessary; people have come of their own accord and in ever greater numbers. With the increasing standard of living, the way of life has been changing especially with young and middle-aged generations which enjoy good food and delicious locally-produced wine and beer. This pleasant relaxed atmosphere can be sensed everywhere in the Old Town. Most visitors who are familiar with the other large cities in the region say that they have not experienced anything like this elsewhere. Everybody finds something in the Old Town to suit his or her taste – an old-fashioned café straight out of Vienna, a restaurant in the latest design like in Milan or a bar in an electricity transformer station with original paintings by Andy Warhol just like in New York. Bratislava selects the latest from the world but at the same time it is proud of its own originals. And what is also important – Bratislava is governed by locals who create this contagious atmosphere. Join them and enjoy life with a glass of excellent local wine and delicious food.

🟥 Quality of Life

Although Bratislavans are very ready to engage animatedly on this topic, Bratislava is in fact a green city, an extensive area of which is parks and especially woodlands, forests and vineyards reaching almost into the city centre. Half of Bratislava is flat and the other half is hilly. These halves even differ in their climate;

while the forests ten minutes from the city centre are still covered in snow, the lowland plains are blooming with spring flowers at the end of March. The presence of woods and dense forests on one side and the Danube with its branches and floodplain forests on the other side provides this city with an exceptional quality of life, which the majority of Bratislavans take for granted as their birthright.

In winter, they take it for granted that they and their children can, in ten minutes by car, get onto a snow-covered slope on a hill beyond the city. In summer, they also take it as given that they can get on a bike by the Danube and, within thirty minutes, be in a raft with their friends confronting white water in one of the best water-sports centres in Europe. In spring, they think it normal that they can sit in a canoe in a branch of the Danube right in the city and go paddling through flooded lowland forests and islands just like on the Amazon. They also think it normal to put on cross-country skis in a valley in the city and go cross-country skiing for tens of kilometres along a prepared trail in beautiful countryside. They also take it as read that 30 minutes by car can have them in a pool in Hungary heated with water from a thermal spring and chatting in Hungarian. And then they regard it as perfectly normal that within another 30 minutes they can be sitting in a wine cellar in Austria and debating agitatedly in German. And, finally, they think it commonplace to drink clean and tasty water originating from deep wells in the Danube islands right in the middle of the city. All of this is absolutely normal - in Bratislava.

1536 - 1783
Pressburg serves as the capital of Hungary

1552 - 1783
Hungarian Crown Jewels guarded in the Castle's Crown Tower

1563 - 1830
Pressburg serves as the coronation town of Hungary

1741
Coronation of Maria Theresa in St Martin's Cathedral

1805
Treaty of Pressburg signed in the Primate's Palace

1811
Devastating fire of the Castle

1919
Pressburg/Pozsony renamed Bratislava and assigned to Czechoslovakia

1948
Communists take power

1989
Velvet Revolution topples communist regime

1993
Bratislava becomes capital of independent Slovakia

2004
Slovakia joins the European Union

2009
Slovakia adopts the euro

Highlights

Highlights in Bratislava

Majestic churches, charming burgher houses and elegant palaces, tiny squares and romantic little streets, and towering over all this, the stately Castle, visible from afar. You can find everything here, but on a small scale. Its human dimensions, friendly atmosphere, musical traditions, irresistible charm, relaxed tempo and its pedestrian centre make this town a well kept secret among people who are looking for something genuine and pleasant. The following places are the minimum you should see before telling your friends at home about your new discovery.

1 Castle

Originally a Gothic castle and the seat of kings, the Castle is without doubt the symbol of Bratislava. It affords a beautiful view over the town and can itself be seen from

a distance of over 30 km. (See pp. 14-17) 🔍 2 CH 27

2 St. Martin's Cathedral

For centuries this former coronation church was the tallest building in the town and it is now its most valuable architectural monument. The crown on the top of the cathedral spire is a reminder of the coronations that took place here. (See pp. 18-21). 🔍 2 CO 27

3 Primate's Palace

This magnificent palace was built as the winter residence of the Hungarian archbishops and now serves as the Town Hall. The splendid rooms can boast of precious English tapestries. (See pp. 22-25) 🔍 2 CV 23

4 Main Square

The "Main Square" in the historical centre is not large, but that makes it all the more pleasant and lively. It is the heart of the Old Town, a meeting place for young couples and con-

certs are held here, as well as popular Christmas fairs. (See pp. 26-27) 🔍 2 CT 24

5 Old Town Hall

This complex of buildings from various periods, harmoniously complementing each other, is to be found in the middle of the Old Town. Here you

an ideal building for the study of architecture and art. (See pp. 30-31) 🔍 2 CT 21

7 Opera House

The elegant building of the Opera House is a living symbol of Bratislava's rich musical traditions. Many people familiar with the town cannot imagine a trip to Bratislava without paying it a visit (See pp. 32-33) 🔍 2 CV 26

8 St. Michael's Gate

One of the dominant landmarks of the Old Town, this is the only gateway in the town's fortifications still standing. There is an interesting museum inside and its balcony offers a delightful view of the Castle. (See pp. 34-35) 🔍 2 CR 20

9 Devín Castle

One of the largest castles in Slovakia is to be found in the west of the city. Nations and civilizations have come and gone here in the course of a thousand years. The fantastic panoramic view is an unforgettable experience. (See pp. 36-37) 🔍 3 FB 9

can breathe in the atmosphere of Bratislava's 600 years of history, with its bright and dark sides. (See pp. 28-29) 🔍 2 CU 23

6 Franciscan Church and Monastery

This, the oldest surviving church in Bratislava, dates back to the end of the 13th century and the many extensions and alterations have made it

1 Castle

The majestic Castle towering 80 m over the Danube has for centuries been the symbol of Bratislava. There have been settlements on the castle hill from time immemorial, thanks to its strategic position. Celts, Romans, Germanic tribes, Slavs and Magyars lived here in turn. The origins of today's Castle go back to the 13th century. From that period originates the so-called Crown Tower, the largest of all the Castle's towers. In the 15th century, the original smaller castle was demolished and replaced with the building which has survived up to today. In the following centuries, the Castle was rebuilt and modified a number of times, and the fortifications were added to it to turn it into a fortress. The last major reconstruction in the 18th century transformed the Castle into a luxury residence in the Baroque style surrounded by elegant gardens in the French style. In 1811, the whole of the Castle complex was totally destroyed in a disastrous fire and abandoned. It was not reconstructed until the second half of the 20th century. In the course of its history the Castle was the seat of the Hungarian monarchs and the crown jewels were kept here. Nowadays it serves mainly as a museum. 🗺 2 CH 27

> ℹ️ Jewels of the early history of Slovakia – daily except for Monday 10.00 – 18.00. History Museum – except for Monday 10.00 – 18.00
> 🔗 snm.sk

1 Castle Well
Beneath the Castle's inner courtyard there is a well, 84 m deep, dating back to 1437. The water level is at a depth of 42 m. In the 18th century it was replaced by a system of water pipes constructed by J. W. Kempelen.

2 Treasure House
The greatest archaeological treasures of Slovakia from the Stone Age to the 13th century are exhibited in the Treasure House. The most valuable object is probably the statue of a woman, 5cm high, made out of a mammoth's tusk and dating from around 22800 BC.

3 Baroque Staircase
As part of reconstruction works undertaken in 1763-65, architect F. A. Hillebrandt had the original staircase demolished, to be replaced by the elegant curved staircase with Rococo decorations that has been preserved to this day.

4 Crown Tower
The Crown Tower is the oldest surviving part of the Castle. Built in the 13th century to defend the older castle, it took its name from the Hungarian crown jewels, which were stored here for most of the time in the period 1552-1783. In the course of your visit to the museum, you can climb up to its top from where a spectacular view is to be had over the entire city.

5 History Museum
The History Museum has several exhibitions at the Castle. The largest of these is an exhibition of historical furniture; this is followed by a collection of silver and another of historical clocks. Several temporary exhibitions are also held here.

6 Original portal
The moment you step through the doorway of the main entrance to the Castle, stop and look

upwards. Just beyond the doors you will see a magnificent Gothic entrance portal with a gateway for pedestrians dating from the 15th century.

7 West Wall
In the 15th century the Castle was deliberately built asymmetrically. The west wing is the longest one, which made it impossible to bom-

9 Theresianum
In 1768 Maria Theresa had a new palace built onto the east wall of the Castle. This became the residence of her daughter Maria Christine and her son-in-law Albert, Duke of Saxe-Teschen. It was destroyed by fire in 1811.

10 Gothic Windows
When the Castle was reconstructed in the 20th century, three Gothic windows were left in the main façade, one above the other, in order to make it easier to imagine the Gothic castle. In the 15th century the Castle had one storey less than it has today.

🎭 "Castle Games"
Every year, during the Cultural Summer festival, a number of different activities take place in the courtyard of the Castle.
Irresistible attractions are performances of plays by Shakespeare having the Castle as their spectacular back-drop, organ concerts as well as days of old masters during which the courtyard is transformed into a busy craft-market.

🔗 bratislava-hrad.sk
🔗 visit.bratislava.sk

bard the other wings. For that reason its outer wall is also the thickest – as much as 7.5m.

8 Chapel
A modern window in the east façade conceals the remains of a chapel and oratory from the middle of the 16th century, the work of Venetian master craftsmen. In its place there was originally an oriel, which was removed in the 17th century when the chapel was walled in. It was only rediscovered during reconstruction work in the 20th century.

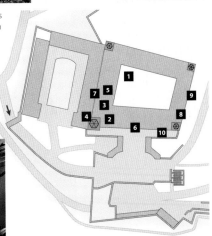

Castle Grounds

1 South Terrace

In the 18th century the space in front of the Castle was reconstructed and the present ceremonial courtyard was created with guardrooms and triumphal arches. The elevated bastion affords a wonderful view over part of the town, the Austrian hills with the little town of Hainburg and its castle.

2 Foundations of a Slavic Basilica

In the 9th century there was a Slavic fortress on the castle hill and during archaeological excavations on the east terrace the remains of a basilica were discovered dating from that century, along with other buildings from the 10th to 12th centuries, whose foundations are marked here in different colours.

3 Sigismund's Gate

The east gate to the Castle, in the direction of the town, is the oldest surviving gateway in

the Castle's fortifications. It dates back to the period of 1430-1440 and was built as part of the Castle that was to serve as the royal seat of Sigismund of Luxemburg.

4 East terrace

The east terrace was formed as early as the 15th century, when a defensive wall was erected. In the 18th century this was reduced in height on account of the view and a French-style garden was laid out. That garden has now been replaced

by a little park and from this wall you get the best view of the town centre.

5 St. Elizabeth

The statue of St. Elizabeth on the east terrace reminds us that the daughter of Hungarian King Andrew II was betrothed here at the age of four to Landgrave Louis IV of Thuringia in 1211. In 1235 she was declared a saint.

6 Stables

The building of the stables from the 18th century was one of the few parts of the Castle that was not destroyed by the great fire in 1811. Its beau-

tiful interior with columns and a vaulted roof is now used by an elegant restaurant. From its terrace there is a splendid view over the historical city centre.

7 West Terrace

In the 18th century a large U-shaped building was built on the site of the filled-in moat. It housed the stables, a kitchen and accommodation for the staff. Its courtyard was used as a summer riding school. The present building is a recently-built copy and it is used by the Parliament.

8 Vienna Gate

The present main gate to the Castle was erected in 1712 to mark the occasion of the coronation of Charles III, father of Maria Theresa, and his visit to the Castle. A chestnut avenue leads from here to the ceremonial courtyard.

9 North Terrace

Here Maria Theresa had a large terraced garden laid out in the French style. A garden pavilion and winter indoor riding school were added to the main palace. There are plans to restore both the garden and the pavilion.

10 Leopold Gate

During the time of the Turkish threat, huge star-shaped fortifications were planned for the Castle. In the end, however, only two bastions were actually built. In 1674 a new gateway was constructed in the western one and named after the emperor, Leopold I.

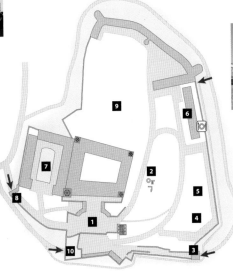

🏰 Maria Theresa and the Castle

Both the city and the Castle owe a great deal to Maria Theresa. During her reign they were at the height of their glory. In 1741 she was crowned queen of Hungary in St. Martin's Cathedral and as Bratislava was at that time the capital of the Hungarian kingdom and near to Vienna, the Castle became her residence. When she ascended the throne the Castle was in a dilapidated state and reconstruction works were necessary to make it a dignified royal residence. In the first years of her reign, however, the queen had to face a number of wars and so, apart from some small alterations she postponed the expensive reconstruction. This was only carried out in 1763-1770 according to the plans of F. A. Hillebrandt and it changed the function of the Castle from a defensive one to an official one. The main palace was rebuilt, numerous new buildings were added and the surroundings as a whole were improved. For the young couple, Albert Duke of Saxe-Teschen, who became viceroy of the Hungarian kingdom, and Maria Christine, Maria Theresa's favourite of her 16 children, the queen had a "new palace" built, which later became known as the "Theresianum". Here Albert found sufficient space for his art collection, which later formed the core of the world-famous Albertina collection in Vienna. The couple spent 15 years in Bratislava and Maria Theresa often visited them. Their presence attracted to the city not only the nobility, who built palaces here, but also many artists and music composers.

◪ St. Martin's Cathedral

St. Martin's Cathedral is without doubt the best-preserved and largest Gothic church in Bratislava. Thanks to its size, it has for centuries dominated the panorama of the city. Work on it began at the beginning of the 14th century, on the site of an earlier Romanesque church. Masons working on St. Stephen's Cathedral in Vienna - Hans Puchsbaum and later Anton Pilgram – contributed to its construction. The church was consecrated in 1452, but subsequent additions to it went on up to 1510. It wasn't until the 18th century that new alterations were undertaken in the Baroque style, which were carried out by leading artists. Further reconstruction works followed in the middle of the 19th century, restoring the church to its original Gothic style. Since then its appearance has remained almost unchanged. 🗺 2 CO 27

> ℹ️ Opening hours for visitors:
> Mon - Sat: 9.00 – 11.30, 13.00 – 17.00
> Sun 14.00 – 16.30, 🌐 dom.fara.sk

◪ North Portal

At the end of the 15th century a chapel dedicated to St. Anne was built in front of the original 14th century north portal. This means it is

now hidden inside the chapel. The present main portal was built at the beginning of the 15th century several metres away from the original entrance.

◪ Steeple

In 1765, following a fire, the original 14th century steeple was given a new Baroque roof designed by F. A. Hillebrandt and surmounted by a model of the Hungarian crown as a symbol of the coronation church. In 1833 the tower was again damaged by fire and the reconstruction work lent it its present appearance. The model of the crown at a height of 85m weighs 300 kg and is 1.5m tall.

◪ Bells

Only Wederin, the largest and oldest of the original six bells has survived. It was cast by Balthasar Herold in 1674. Weighing 2.5 tons, this bell is one of the most historically valuable in Europe. The other bells were melted down during the First World War. In 2000 St. Martin's Cathedral was given five new bells as a gift from the capitals of the neighbouring countries.

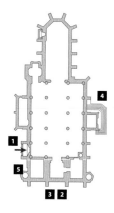

◪ South Entrance

The last part of the church to be constructed in the Gothic style was the south entrance, dating from 1510. It is ascribed to the workshop of Anton Pilgram, a mason who worked on St. Stephen's Cathedral in Vienna. The side entrance already bears signs of the Renaissance style that was to follow.

Coronations

After the Turkish occupation of a large part of the country in the 16th century, Pressburg (today's Bratislava) was named coronation city of the Hungarian kings. St. Martin's Cathedral became the coronation church and the first coronation took place here in 1563. Eleven kings and 8 royal wives were crowned here before 1830. All the monarchs crowned here were from the Habsburg dynasty. On the eve of the coronation, the crown and royal insignia were brought from the Castle, where they were usually kept under guard, to the sacristy in the cathedral. In the morning the monarch would set out from the Castle in a ceremonial procession heralded by pealing bells, cannon fire and trumpet fanfares. After the coronation and mass the procession paraded through the city to the Franciscan Church, where the king knighted chosen members of the nobility (See p. 28). The coronation tradition always comes to life the last weekend in June. This is the highlight of the city's festivities and every year it attracts tens of thousands of visitors to Bratislava, where they become part of the magnificent historical ceremony, knights' tournaments and celebrations (See p. 68).

5 Little Tower with a Toilet

In the past the church was part of the city's fortifications. A short way from the main entrance to the church, on its north-western corner, there is a little tower jutting out from the wall, with a staircase inside. It dates from the beginning of the 15th century and in its corner it has a well-preserved Mediaeval WC with an opening over the former moat.

Church Concerts

Every year in August and September the Cathedral is host to an Organ Festival on the new organ built by Gerald Woehl.

Interior of St. Martin's Cathedral

bytery proved to be too short and it was demolished. Soon afterwards work was begun on the construction of a more spacious one, more richly decorated than the main nave. Completed in 1487, the vaults bear the coats-of-arms of all those who helped finance the building work. In

1 Chapel of St. John the Almoner

On account of the danger posed by the Turks, in 1530 the remains of St. John the Almoner and other articles of value were transferred for safekeeping from Buda to St. Martin's Cathedral. When the cathedral was reconstructed in the Baroque style according to Georg Raphael Donner's design, a Baroque chapel was

built in 1732, where the remains of this 7th century saint were placed. It was also intended to serve as the funeral chapel of Archbishop Emmerich Eszterházy himself, who financed the reconstruction.

2 Statue of St. Martin

After the completion of the Chapel of St. John the Almoner, the presbytery was reconstructed in Baroque style and Georg Raphael Donner designed a monumental high altar. The focal point of the altar was a sculpture of St. Martin on a horse sharing his cloak with a beggar. In contrast to the tradition of depicting St. Martin as a Roman soldier, Donner gave him the features of the archbishop in a Hungarian uniform. This lead sculpture is the only part of the whole altar to have survived and it now stands in the corner of the main nave.

3 Presbytery

After the cathedral's consecration in 1452, the pres-

the 19th century an incomplete list of the kings and queens who had been crowned in the cathedral was painted on the northern wall.

4 Chapel of St. Anne

In the second half of the 15th century, at the same time as the new Presbytery was being built, Hans Puchsbaum also constructed the Chapel of St. Anne

✉ Georg Raphael Donner in Bratislava

When in the 18th century a patron of the arts, Archbishop Imrich Eszterházy, decided to refurbish the interior of St. Martin's Cathedral in the Baroque style, he invited the most famous Central European artists of those times to contribute to it. One of these was the sculptor Georg Raphael Donner, who moved to Bratislava for this purpose and lived here for 10 years. The archbishop set up a studio in his summer residence (now the seat of the Slovak Government), which produced many famous works not only for Bratislava, but also for Vienna (See pp. 40-41).

🔖 Musical Traditions of St. Martin's Cathedral

St. Martin's Cathedral is closely associated with the rich musical traditions of the city. Naturally, the greatest musical performances took place on the occasion of the coronations. Felix Mendelsohn-Bartholdy wrote enthusiastically about his impressions of the last coronation in 1830 in a letter to his brother. St. Martin's Church Music Society founded in 1833 attracted renowned conductors, thanks to whom the most demanding compositions were performed. These included Mozart's Requiem in 1834 and a year later Beethoven's Missa Solemnis. In 1840 Franz Liszt himself conducted the local orchestra for the first time; later he became a member of the Society and was a frequent visitor to the city. He came here to be present at a performance of his Esztergom Mass and in 1884 he conducted his Coronation Mass in St. Martin's Cathedral. The last of the Society's famous conductors was the composer Alexander Albrecht, a pupil of Béla Bartók.

🔖 Crowned Monarchs and their Wives

1. .... 👑 Maximilian 1563
2. .... 👑 Maria 1563
   (wife of Maximilian)
3. .... 👑 Rudolf 1576
4. .... 👑 Matthias II 1608
5. .... 👑 Anna 1613
   (wife of Matthias II)
6. .... 👑 Ferdinand II 1618
7. .... 👑 Eleonora 1622
   (wife of Ferdinand II)
8. .... 👑 Maria Anna 1638
   (1st wife of Ferdinand III)
9. .... 👑 Ferdinand IV 1647
10. .... 👑 Maria Eleonora 1655
    (3rd wife of Ferdinand III)
11. .... 👑 Leopold I 1655
12. .... 👑 Joseph I 1687
13. .... 👑 Charles III 1712
14. .... 👑 Elizabeth Christine 1714
    (wife of Charles III)
15. .... 👑 Maria Theresa 1741
16. .... 👑 Leopold II 1790
17. .... 👑 Maria Ludovica 1808
    (3rd wife of Francis I)
18. .... 👑 Karoline Auguste 1825
    (4th wife of Francis I)
19. .... 👑 Ferdinand V 1830

on the north side of the cathedral. The highly prized portal inside is the original church portico from the first half of the 14th century. Also, the cathedral's oldest sculpture - the gravestone of Bratislava Provost and Vice-Chancellor Georg Schomberg of the first university - Academia Istropolitana from 1470 – is to be found here. From the chapel, there is also the entrance into the cathedral crypts.

5 Baptismal Font

The bronze font is the oldest surviving part of the Gothic furnishings. It was presented to the cathedral in 1409 by the city's mayor, Ulrich Rauchenwarter. Its lid is neo-Gothic and dates from 1878.

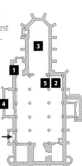

🔖 St. John the Almoner

Originating from Cyprus and highly-respected by Cypriots, St. John the Almoner became the Patriarch of the Greek Christians in Alexandria. He died in Cyprus in 619. His remains were presented to Hungarian king Matthias Corvinus as the gift of a Turkish sultan in the 15th century and were deposited in the royal chapel in Buda. In 1530, in order to protect the remains from the Turks, they were transferred to St. Martin's Cathedral. Undoubtedly, Cypriots would like to have him returned to the island of his birth.

◳ Primate's Palace

In the last years of Bratislava's golden age, just before it lost its status as capital of the Hungarian kingdom, Archbishop Cardinal Joseph Batthyany ordered the building of the largest and grandest palace in the city. This was designed by the Viennese architect Melchior Hefele in the style of French Neoclassicism and was completed in 1781. It became the winter residence of the Esztergom archbishop and on occasion it provided accommodation for monarchs after the coronation ceremony. Since 1903 the palace has served as the Town Hall. The grand first floor is open to the public and the greatest attraction it has to offer is a set of precious royal English tapestries dating from the 17th century. ◳ 2 CV 23

❶ Putti

In the middle of the façade, above a first floor window, there are two playful putti holding the letters C and I. These are the initials of Maria

Theresa's Latin motto – Clementia et Iustitia, which the archbishop also took as his own.

the original fresco by the Austrian painter F. A. Maulbertsch.

❸ Allegorical Statues and the Coat-of-Arms

The roof of the palace is decorated with statues and vases. The statues represent virtues and civic duties. Crowning the tympanum is the archbishop's coat-of-arms and a large model of a cardinal's hat.

❹ Memorial Plaque

In the entrance to the palace on the right there is a memorial plaque from 1905 recalling a historical event

❷ Tympanum

The large mosaic in the tympanum by Ernest Zmeták depicts the allegory of supervising the fulfilment of the Ten Commandments. In the middle of the 20th century it replaced

– the signing of the Pressburg Treaty (Le traité de Pressbourg) in 1805 in the palace's Hall of Mirrors.

5 St. George's Fountain

The fountain depicting St. George slaying the dragon, situated in the inner courtyard, comes from the 17th

🎣 The Treaty of Pressburg

Following the Battle of Austerlitz, also known as the Battle of Three Emperors – Austrian Emperor Francis I and Russian Emperor Alexander I fighting on the one side and Napoleon I (Bonaparte) on the other – what is known as the Treaty of Pressburg (Le traité de Pressbourg) was signed on 26th December 1805 in the Hall of Mirrors in the Primate's Palace. The treaty was signed on behalf of the French by Foreign Secretary Talleyrand and by Prince von Liechtenstein for the Austrians. As a result of his defeat in one of the bloodiest battles of the Napoleonic wars, the Austrian emperor lost a large part of his territory, while Napoleon was at the height of his power. In memory of the place where the treaty was signed, the road around the Arc de Triomphe in Paris was named "rue de Pressbourg".

In diesem Hause wurde nach der Schlacht bei Austerlitz am 26ten Dezember 1805 der Pressburger Frieden geschlossen, welcher dem Reiche des österreichischen Kaisers Franz den I. Venezien, Istrien Dalmatien und Tirol entriss, den Kaiser Napoleon hingegen auf den Gipfel seiner Macht erhob.

Die Friedensurkunde wurde seitens des französischen Kaisers von Talleyrand, seitens des Kaisers von Österreich hingegen von Lichtenstein unterzeichnet. Zum Gedächtnis des grossen Weltereignisses wurde diese Inschrifttafel bei Gelegenheit der hundertjährigen Wiederkehr des Tages von der Bevölkerung Pressburgs, im Jahre 1905 in die Wand dieses Hauses eingelassen.

century. Originally it was in the garden of the archbishop's summer residence, which is now the seat of the Slovak Government, and it was only transferred to this courtyard in the 20th century.

> ℹ️ Open daily except for Monday: 10.00 – 17.00. The Hall of Mirrors is used for concerts. Masses are held in St. Ladislas' Chapel on Sundays and holidays at 8.00.
> 🌐 visit.bratislava.sk

Interior of the Palace

1 Entrance Hall

The first room above the large staircase is the entrance hall, with portraits of members of the Habsburg dynasty and Cardinal Batthyany, for whom the palace was built. The most interesting portrait is one dating from 1742 of Maria Theresa as Queen of Hungary.

2 Hall of Mirrors

This hall is the largest room in the palace. The mirrors on either side were designed to enlarge the hall optically and diffuse the daylight. Coronation balls were held here in the past and the hall also witnessed the signing of the Pressburg Peace Treaty. Nowadays it is used for sessions of the municipal parliament and as a concert hall.

3 Set of Tapestries

A set of six royal English tapestries from the 17th century can be seen hanging in the state rooms. They depict the Greek legend of the tragic love of the priestess Hero and Leander.

One stormy night Leander was drowned when attempting to swim across the Hellespont, a dangerous strait dividing Europe and Asia, in order to meet his loved one.

4 St. Ladislas' Chapel

Apart from a small entrance portal from the inner courtyard there is nothing to suggest that

🎗 English Tapestries

The tapestries in the Primate's Palace are one of the city's most valuable artistic treasures and at the same time a mystery yet to be solved. This set of six tapestries comes from the oldest English royal factory in Mortlake, London, which was managed by Sir Francis Crane. Established in 1619 by King James I, it employed Flemish weavers. The tapestries are hand made and they were woven for King Charles I after 1632. At the time of the English Civil War, following the death of Charles I, they fell into the hands of the Republicans, who probably sold them to someone in France. No one knows how and when they found their way to Bratislava. They were discovered only by chance in 1903 during reconstruction works, after the archbishop had sold the palace to the town. It remains a mystery why they were hidden and for how long. There are two events that come into consideration – the capitulation of the town after the French siege in 1809 and the revolution in 1848-49. Only three sets of the oldest English royal tapestries in the world have survived more or less intact. One of them is here and the other two are to be found in Liverpool (Port Sunlight – Lady Lever Art Gallery) and in the Swedish royal castle of Drotningholm near Stockholm.

inside there is an artistic treasure stretching the height of the whole building. The chapel is oval in shape and its ceiling is decorated with a large fresco – the miracle of St. Ladislas, by the Austrian painter F. A. Maulbertsch. The chapel can be seen during a tour of the first floor from the archbishop's private oratory.

5 Picture Gallery

The northern wing of the first floor, with windows overlooking the square, has five reception rooms.

There are mirrors facing each other at opposite ends of the rooms, creating the illusion of endless

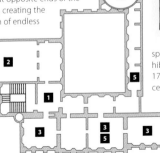

space. Apart from the tapestries, there is an exhibition of Italian paintings from the 16th and 17th centuries and in the west wing of 17th century Dutch and Flemish paintings.

4 Main Square

The heart of the Old Town is an even-sided square (Hlavné námestie), dating right back to the 13th century. From the outset it was the focal point of life in the town – markets, executions, protest gatherings, as well as entertainments and artists' performances all took place here. Its appearance changed over the centuries. In the Middle Ages it was overlooked by fortified houses with towers, later to be replaced by palaces. Since the 15th century it has had stone paving and in the 16th century a fountain was added to enhance its beauty. Nowadays it is the scene of markets, concerts or performances by artists and the fountain is a popular meeting place. From a chair in one of the typical cafes you can not only admire architecture spanning a period of 600 years, but also enjoy the traditional bustle and atmosphere of the Old Town. Here you are sitting right at the heart of things. 2 CT 24

1 Jeszenák Palace

This 18th century palace with a little courtyard was built on the foundations of a Mediaeval house. On its corner you can see the striking, richly decorated coat-of-arms of its owner. On the ground floor there is one of the best-known

cafes in the city – Kaffee Mayer, which has been here since 1873.

2 Romanesque House

The large green building on the corner of the square, next to the Old Town Hall, was originally a 13th century Romanesque house with a defensive tower. In the 15th century it was renovated in Gothic style. The supporting pillar at the corner dates from this period. It took on its present appearance at the end of the 18th century.

3 Old Town Hall

The original town hall is the dominating feature in the square on account of its tower. It is made up of several buildings joined together, dating from the 15th to 20th centuries, which were gradually acquired by the city. It now houses the Bratislava City Museum and markets and concerts are held in its charming little enclosed courtyard. (See pp. 28-29).

4 Viceroy's Palace

The palace was constructed in 1762 by joining two buildings to become the residence of the Viceroy. It is a typical example of the austere architecture of state buildings in that period. Nowadays it serves as accommodation during state visits. For comparison – the neighbouring palace for a member of the nobility was built in the same year.

5 Kutscherfeld Palace

The palace was built for Leopold von Kutscherfeld on the site of three older houses in 1762. It is one of the most impressive Rococo palaces in the city. The building was later bought by the Eszterházy family and in 1847 the Russian pianist Anton Rubinstein lived and composed here as their guest.

6 "Green House"

Way back in the 15th century there was a tavern here called Grünstübl, on account of its paintings, in which green was the predominant colour.

The local wine was served from barrels here, as illustrated in the relief with a biblical motif on the roof. Regional parliaments held sessions in the building's spacious rooms and theatrical performances were organized, which were even attended by the queen, Maria Theresa.

7 Napoleonic Soldier

In front of Kutscherfeld Palace, now the seat of the

French Embassy, there stands a bronze statue of a Napoleonic soldier leaning on a bench. Most tourists cannot resist the temptation to be photographed with him. The sculptor, Juraj Meliš, could not suppress his Slovak humour and depicted him barefoot and with his hat falling on his nose.

8 Art Nouveau House

The youngest building in the square is an Art Nouveau bank building erected in 1904. On the ground floor, in the former main hall of the bank with its beautiful Art Nouveau mosaics, there is now an elegant cafe. The build-

ing was designed by a renowned Budapest architect, Edmund Lechner, who is the author of the best-known Art Nouveau building in Bratislava – the "Blue Church". (See p. 42.)

9 Maximilian Fountain

In the middle of the square there stands the oldest surviving fountain in Bratislava. It was made in 1572 by Andreas Luttringer from nearby Bad Deutsch-Altenburg on the orders of King Maximilian. In the 18th century, as a result of protests from shocked inhabitants, the original decoration with boys urinating was exchanged for the present one with boys holding fish. The original is now to be found in the courtyard of the Ruttkay Palace. (See pp. 44 and 46)

10 Markets

As in former times, now too, markets are held in the square. In the period between Easter and the end of October there is a market for souvenirs and handmade products and between the first day of Advent and Christmas there is a traditional Christmas Market, which is one of Bratislava's greatest winter attractions.

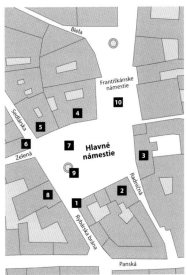

5 Old Town Hall

As elsewhere in Europe, in Bratislava, too, the town hall was the focal point of the city and reflected its wealth. However, as the Main Square was too small for it to be built in its centre, the town decided to buy an already-existing edifice in the square. The 14th century house of Mayor Jacob, bought by the town, is overlooked to this day by its original defence tower. In the centuries that followed, the town acquired all the neighbouring houses and joined them together. The result is a splendid complex of various buildings from different periods, complementing each other in a harmonious way, and ideal for the study of architecture. Although the Old Town Hall no longer serves the purpose implied by its name, it still makes a considerable contribution to the cultural life of the Old Town. 🔍 2 CU 23

> ℹ️ Bratislava City Museum open daily except for
> Monday: 10.00 – 17.00 Sat-Sun 11.00 – 18.00.
> ⮞ muzeum.bratislava.sk

1 Tower

The tower, originally designed for defence, comes from the 14th century and belongs to Mayor Jacob's rectangular house behind it. There were several such houses with towers in Bratislava in the Middle Ages. In the centuries that followed, the tower was reconstructed and its present appearance dates back to 1733. Its balcony, which can be reached through the museum, affords the most beautiful view of the Old Town and the Castle and should not be missed by any visitor to the city.

2 Cannon Ball

As a reminder of the French siege of the town in 1805 and again in 1809, a cannon ball was built into the wall next to a Gothic window on the first floor of the tower. Seven of them have been preserved to this day in façades in the historical centre. At that time the town suffered more damage than during the Second World War.

3 Oriel

The Renaissance oriel next to the tower was built in the 16th century. In the 19th century it was adapted to the neo-Gothic style and its little roof was covered with colourful glazed tiles.

4 Portrait of a Man

To the right of the oriel in the main façade there is a painted portrait of a bearded man. As it is still unclear who it depicts, it has been a source of conjecture and legend. Some people suppose that it is the Greek lawgiver Solon. Legend has it that it was an alderman who was carried away by the Devil as a punishment for perjury.

5 Inner Courtyard

Beyond the Gothic passageway there is one of the most beautiful of Bratislava's enclosed courtyards. A 14th century house with well-preserved Gothic windows on the first floor forms its northern side. In 1581 a Renaissance arcade was built on to it. The western side was added in the 18th century and the southern and eastern, although they look older, only in 1912.

🎭 Cultural Events

Throughout the year, thanks to its very special atmosphere, as well as its good acoustics, the inner courtyard of the Old Town Hall is witness to various cultural events. Arts and crafts fairs, theatrical performances, folk costume shows, concerts or opportunities to taste the wine from the vineyards around Bratislava – all these enable you to enjoy the particular charm of this town.
➼ *visit.bratislava.sk*

ube was regulated and the embankments constructed.

7 Museum

Ever since 1868 the Old Town Hall has housed a Bratislava City Museum, which has gradually spread into all the buildings. The attractive original halls are worth a visit, as well as the interesting temporary exhibitions. During a sightseeing tour it is not only possible to go out onto the balcony of the tower,

but also to enter the former dungeons and find out what methods of torture were used at one time in the past.

8 Portal and Passageway

The portal and well-preserved Gothic passageway leading to the inner courtyard originated during reconstruction works in 1442. Various metal measuring vessels were fixed to the portal, so that anyone could check whether the goods they bought on the market were the correct quantity.

6 Watermark

On the lower part of the tower, about 1m above the pavement, there is a little plaque with a date. This was the height reached by the waters of the Danube when it flooded the town in 1850. In the past, floods were not uncommon in the town, until the end of the 19th century, when the Dan-

9 East Façade

When additions were made to the Town Hall in 1912, a new east wing with a neo-Gothic façade was also built facing onto the Primate's Square (Primaciálne námestie). The eye is drawn to the roof, which is covered with what

were then very fashionable glazed tiles in a variety of colours.

10 Lunar Globe

Since the 16th century there has been a lunar globe high up on the tower, just under the clock on the Main Square side. In the past it used to turn with the clock and show the phases of the moon.

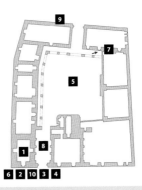

6 Franciscan Church and Monastery

The Franciscans settled in Bratislava in the 13th century. Around 1250 they began to build the present church, which was consecrated in 1297, making it the oldest surviving church in the town. The presbytery and the outer walls of the church from this period are still standing, but the vaulting is in the Renaissance style, the original Gothic vaulting having collapsed following earthquakes at the end of the 16th century. The 18th century saw the addition of the present main façade in the Baroque style. The church and monastery played an important role in the life of the town: it was here that the mayor was elected and the Parliament held its sessions, and in 1526 Ferdinand Habsburg was elected King of Hungary. 🔍 2 CT 21

1 Pietà Altar

The side altars in the church, dating from the first half of the 18th century, feature pictures of the saints. The focal point of the only altar on the northern side is a precious Gothic sandstone statue of the Pietà from the beginning of the 15th century.

2 Tower

A tower with interesting gargoyles was built in the middle of the 15th century, but having been damaged was replaced by a copy at the end of the 19th century. The original is to be found in the Janko Kráľ Park. (See pp. 44-45). In the past the "Beer Bell" in the tower used to announce the opening and closing of the taverns.

3 Monastery

The original 13th century Minorite monastery, which was burned down, was replaced in the 15th century by a new Gothic one. After the earthquake in the 16th century it was rebuilt and the existing cloister was constructed around the courtyard. The monastery was subsequently reconstructed a number of times. The courtyard affords the best view of the church's Gothic tower.

4 Chapel of St. John the Evangelist

In the second half of the 14th century Mayor Jacob's family had a two-storey funeral chapel built on the site of an older one. It was

modelled on la Sainte-Chapelle in Paris, the chapel of the French kings. It is one of the best examples of High Gothic in Slovakia.

5 Loretto Chapel

The Baroque chapel at the corner of the church dates back to 1708. It is a simplified imitation of the Marian chapel in the Italian town of Loretto. It was established by the Palatine Paul Eszterházy, whose coat-of-arms can be seen in the façade.

6 St. Rosalia Chapel

The chapel can be reached from the rear of the courtyard and originally was dedicated to St. Sebastian. The outer walls are the original Gothic ones, but the vaults are from the beginning of the 17th century. The whole of the interior dates from the 17th and 18th centuries.

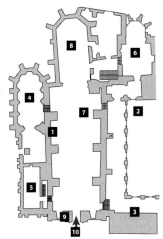

7 Pulpit

The interesting Rococo pulpit on the south side of the church was designed by Ludwig Gode, Georg Raphael Donner's successor, in 1756.

8 Presbytery

This is the oldest part of the church to have survived intact from the 13th century, with the original painted decorations restored. The high altar comes from 1720-30 and large bronze candlesticks stand on either side of it.

✉ The Franciscan Church and the Coronations

After the coronation in St. Matin's Cathedral, the king and his retinue made their way through the streets to the Franciscan Church. Here he bestowed the title of Knight of the Golden Spur on chosen nobles. Then the procession continued through St. Michael's Gate to outside the town walls. (See. pp. 68-69).

9 Portal

When the new main façade was built in the 18th century, the original magnificent 13th century portal was walled in. This was rediscovered during recent reconstruction works and restored in its original colours.

10 Main Façade

The church's façade was designed in the Baroque style by the builder Lucca de Schramm in 1745-46. This was the last extensive alteration to the church. A statue of the Madonna by Joseph Sartory was placed above the portal.

🟦7 Opera House

The neo-Renaissance building of the Slovak National Theatre's opera house was built in 1884-86 as the Municipal Theatre. It is the work of Viennese architects Fellner and Helmer, who specialised in theatre buildings. The new building replaced the older Municipal Theatre from 1776, which was no longer suitable. A performance of the opera Bánk Bán by Ferenc Erkel marked its official opening. The Slovak National Theatre was founded in 1920 and under the management of Oskar Nedbal the opera achieved a high standard. Thanks to its renown and first-class artists, the opera here is a secret delight for connoisseurs of classical music. 🖻 2 CV 26

> ℹ️ Performances start at 19.00; performances for children in the morning.
> Box-office:
> Mon-Fri: 8.00–19.00, Sat: 9.00 – 13.00
> ⮑ snd.sk

🟦1 Fellner and Helmer

The theatre in Bratislava is one of many buildings by this successful pair of Viennese architects, who designed theatres in Budapest, Vienna, Zurich, Berlin and many other European cities.

🟦2 Busts of Playwrights and Composers

In the oval niches in the façade there are busts of Goethe, Mozart, Katona, Liszt and Shakespeare. In the 1930s they were removed and only recently returned after restoration to their original position.

🟦3 Fountain

Ganymede's fountain (1888) was designed by a native of Bratislava, Viktor Tilgner, the author of Mozart's memorial in Vienna. It depicts the Greek legend of Ganymede, who on account of his unusual beauty was carried

room accessible during the intervals in a performance and a loggia with interesting frescoes.

🟦5 Terrace

The terrace outside the loggia can be reached through the reception room. From here there is a splendid view of the whole square in front of the opera house. In summer, fanfare concerts can be heard from here.

🟦6 Auditorium

After alterations designed to increase the comfort of visitors, the opera's auditorium has a capacity of 611 seats, which is fewer than originally.

off by Zeus, disguised as an eagle. The fountain is decorated with sculptures of fish and animals living in the River Danube.

🟦4 Reception Room

On the first floor there is an elegant reception

7 Oskar Nedbal

This famous Czech composer and conductor was the opera company's director from 1923-30. He was a pupil of Antonín Dvořák and later principal conductor of the Czech Philharmonic Orchestra. In 1907-19 he lived in Vienna, where he conducted the Tonkünstlerorchester and was kapellmeister in the Volksoper. The opera in Bratislava achieved a high standard and attracted many famous artists.

8 Famous Artists

The opera experienced its first glorious era between the two world wars. Stars such as Rose Pauly and Emmy Destinn appeared here and performances were conducted by such famous names as Pietro Mascagni or Richard Strauss.

Slovak opera singers such as Lucia Popp, Edita Grúberova, Peter Dvorský, Gabriela Beňačková or Sergej Kopčák, who debuted here in the second half of the 20th century, have become world-famous stars.

📖 History of the Opera

Although there had been theatre performances here since the Middle Ages, it was only in the 18th century that the opera became popular. At that time opera theatres in the courtyards of the nobility achieved a high standard and operas by Haydn and Mozart were great favourites. As the town didn't have a permanent stage or the funds to finance one, in 1774 -1776 Count Csáky had a Municipal Theatre built at his own expense in front of the Rybárska brána gateway. Dramas by Lessing, Schiller, Goethe and Shakespeare were performed there and in the 19th century well-known works by Rossini, Donnizetti, Verdi and Wagner. At the end of the 19th century operetta outstripped opera in popularity and works by Offenbach, Lehár and Kálmán were staged.

9 Ballet

The Slovak National Theatre is also well known for its ballet company. In the period between the wars it was headed by Achille Viscusi, who contributed a great deal to its quality. The present ballet company is made up of talented young dancers from Slovakia and abroad.

10 Opera House Ball

Every year a ball is held in the Opera House for

the Bratislava elite. It is organised by one of the opera company's sponsors and is only by invitation. On this occasion the seats are removed from the auditorium in order to make room for a dance floor.

⑧ St. Michael's Gate

The only one of the original four gateways in the town fortifications still standing is the northern one, St. Michael's Gate. It was built in the 14th century and was named after the Gothic church of St. Michael, which was situated outside the fortifications and was pulled down in the 16th century on account of the Turks. Additions were made to the gateway a number of times until it took on its present appearance in the 18th century, shortly before the town's fortifications were almost entirely demolished. Thanks to its tall, onion-shaped dome, the tower over the gateway is one of the landmarks of the Old Town. Its balcony affords a panoramic view of the castle hill, the city's roofs and towers, as well as of the garden suburb in the Carpathian foothills. 🔍 2 CR 20

> ℹ️ Open daily except for Monday: 10.00 – 17.00;
> Sat – Sun: 11.00 – 18.00;
> 🖥️ muzeum.bratislava.sk

① Bridge Across the Moat

The present stone footbridge decorated with statues of St. John Nepomuck and the Archangel Michael that leads across the moat to the gateway was built in 1727. It replaced an older wooden drawbridge. From the bridge there is a good view of the former moat below it, as well as of a section of the town walls.

② Barbican

For strategic reasons a barbican was built in front of the gateway in the 15th century. The approach turned off at right angles, thus protecting the gateway itself from cannon fire. The barbican had its own gate, which was rebuilt in 1712, taking on its present appearance with two passageways – for vehicles and for pedestrians. On the outer side you can still see the openings for the ropes of the drawbridge.

③ Tower

The lower, rectangular part of the tower with its passageway comes from the first half of the 14th century. In 1511-1513 the octagonal superstructure was added and in 1753-58 it received its present Baroque dome roof.

④ Archangel Michael

When the last part of the tower was added in the 18th century, a copper statue of Archangel Michael slaying a dragon was placed on the top of the tower at a height of 50m. At that time contemporary documents were stored in the head of the statue, which are added to every time repairs are made.

⑤ Watchtower Balcony

When on a tour of the museum, from the last floor you can go out onto the balcony encircling the tower, which offers panoramic views of the centre of Bratislava. The most beautiful of these is in the direction of the castle hill and the garden suburb on the hillsides.

⑥ Museum

Nowadays the tower houses a Museum of Arms and Town Fortifications, with exhibits on the different floors showing the development of various arms from the Central European re-

🔊 Watchman

A watchman used to live in the tower and it was his duty to blow a trumpet or ring the bells to announce a fire in the town and to look after the clock. There are still two bells in the tower and the trumpet is to be found in the museum there.

gate, which was demolished – like the rest of the town outside the walls – for fear of Turkish attacks in the 16th century. The building materials thus gained were used to strengthen the town's defences.

9 Coats-of-Arms

There are coats-of-arms on both sides of the tower. The stone one on the upper, northern side was put there when the tower was added to in 1511-1513. The lead coat-of-arms on the side facing Michalská ulica recalls the last reconstruction of the tower, completed in 1758.

10 Narrow House

The little house adjoining the tower on the upper, northern side is generally considered to be the narrowest in the town. From the front it really does seem that it is only the width of the door. However, it is in fact the same house that is next to the gateway on the Michalská ulica side.

gion. A little cannon in front of the entrance draws your attention to the museum.

7 Zero Point

Below the gate is a mark showing the cardinal points and the distance of European and other world capitals from Bratislava.

8 Tombstone

When looking from the street known as Michalská ulica, notice the pink stone on the left side of the tower where the corner stone should be, at the height of the roof of the next house. It is a fragment of a Gothic tombstone from an old cemetery outside the

9 Devín Castle

Perched on the top of a high rock overlooking the confluence of the Danube and Morava rivers, only 10 km west of the centre of Bratislava, stands Devín Castle. It is one of the most important historical and archaeological localities in Central Europe and provides excellent evidence of the history of the settlement of present-day Slovakia. Thanks to its strategic position, the castle hill was inhabited back in primeval times and it was held or fought over by many nations. Celts settled here, Romans used it to keep a watch on their borders, Slavs built a formidable fortress, and later a castle guarded for centuries the western frontier of the Hungarian kingdom. It was taken by force many times, but it was always repaired and strengthened. In the end it was not destroyed in battle, but blown up for no reason by French troops in 1809. If you are not impressed by several thousand years of history, you will still be charmed by the natural scenery and the fantastic view (See p. 122). 🔍 3 FB 9

1 Maiden's Tower

In the 16th century, apart from other things, the Castle's defences were improved. On the southern side a wall with several bastions was built around the castle rock, leading right down to the

confluence of the rivers. A little watchtower was also constructed on the top of a sharp, high rock overlooking the water, which on account of a legend later came to be known as the Maiden's Tower.

2 Confluence

From the upper part of the Castle you can clearly see the grey waters of the Danube swallowing up the brown water of the River Morava. As at this point the border passes down the middle of the Danube and Morava rivers, the opposite bank is already in Austria. Until 1989 the "Iron Curtain" ran along here and a barbed wire fence cut off access to the water.

3 West Gate

The western defences of the Castle from the River Morava side date back to the 15th century. At that time the main gate to the Castle was also built and it is the one of best preserved. It was protected by two towers and a moat, over which there was a drawbridge.

> ℹ️ Open: May–October, daily except for Monday: 10.00 – 17.00, Sat – Sun: 11.00 – 18.00. From under the New Bridge bus Nr. 29 takes you right under the castle. 🚌 muzeum.bratislava.sk

Christian building to be discovered to the north of the Danube, which in those times formed the

limes – the frontier of the Roman Empire. Devín was an important strategic point protecting the nearby town of Carnuntum from the barbarians.

4 Roman Chapel

Beside the West Gate there are the uncovered foundations of an early Christian chapel from the 4th century which served the Roman legionaries. It is the oldest

5 Slavic Basilica

In the 9th century Devín became an important centre of the first state formation of the western Slavs – Great Moravia. A large fortress with a church was built on the top

🏛 "Castle Games"

One of the greatest attractions for both children and adults is an event known as the Castle Games, organized here at weekends during the summer months. This festival of historical fencing, dancing and music, accompanied by an arts and crafts fair, at least partially revives the Mediaeval life of the Castle.
➲ *visit.bratislava.sk*

of the hill. Here you can find the reconstructed foundations of this church and a small model of it.

6 Museum

Part of the middle castle houses a museum exhibition documenting the history of the Castle and presenting the most precious archaeological finds from ancient times up to the Middle Ages.

7 Middle Castle

In the 16th century, when the Báthory family were owners of the Castle, a new palace was erected in the middle castle. In comparison with the high Gothic roofs, its roof was flat and had a typical semi-arched attic gable which has partially survived to the present day.

8 Well

In the inner courtyard of the middle castle, there is a reconstructed well from

the 15th century. Its depth is 53 m. When it was cleaned out, a number of articles demonstrating the everyday life of those times were found.

9 Upper Castle

The first records of a Mediaeval Castle come from 1233. Its oldest part was built on the top of the rocky hill. The main part of the upper castle consisted of a hexagonal residential tower, three floors high. Here you will understand the enormous strategic importance of Devin. On a clear day you can see Vienna and the eastern Alps from this spot.

10 Caves

Use was made of the caves running through the whole of the rocky hill by people in ancient times and later by the Romans and the Slavs. The caves were gradually modified and later joined to the upper castle and used for storing foodstuffs. A section is open to the public and it houses an interesting exhibition about the history of the Castle.

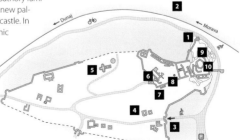

Sights

Palaces and historical buildings

1 Good Shepherd

The picturesque House of the Good Shepherd was built on a tiny plot of ground in the seventeen-sixties. Its name derives from the statue of a little shepherd in the corner. The building is so narrow that it has only one room on each of its four floors. The House is an example of fine Rococo architecture unique in Central Europe. A

painted blank window on the east side of the building is an interesting feature. In its interior, the Museum of Clocks will charm you with its atmosphere of the ticking of many historical clocks. (See pp. 60 and 61). 🔍 2 CN 26

2 De Pauli Palace

The palace was built in 1775-76 for Count Leopold de Pauli on the site of an older royal house. It was the only palace situated within the city walls which had both a courtyard and a garden. At the end of the garden stands the Rococo pavilion in which the nine-year old Franz Liszt began his musical career by performing before local aristocrats. Today, the palace forms a part of the University Library and concerts are given in Liszt's garden. (See pp. 48 and 49). 🔍 2 CQ 24

3 Royal Hungarian Chamber

This, the highest Hungarian financial institution, existed in Bratislava from 1531. The older outmoded buildings were demolished and replaced by the palace designed by the court ar-

chitect Martinelli in 1753-1756. In 1772, the palace was extended by another building with the passageway designed by F. A. Hillebrandt. In 1802-1848, the sessions of the Hungarian Parliament were held here and it was here that serfdom was abolished

in 1848. Nowadays, it houses the University Library. 🔍 2 CR 22

4 Archbishop's Summer Palace

The palace was commissioned by Archbishop Forgách in 1614 in an area of vineyards, as a summer residence for the archbishops of Esztergom. In the middle of

the 17th century, a rare, geometrical-style botanical garden filled with exotic plants and adorned with a number of statues and fountains was established at the rear of the palace. Georg Raphael Donner had his studio in the palace in 1729-39. (See pp.18 and 19). In 1761-65 the palace was rebuilt in the Baroque style and the garden redesigned in the French style. In the 19th century the garden was transformed into an English park. Today, the palace is the Office of the Slovak Government. 🔍 2 CV 4

5 Grassalkovich Palace

The palace was commissioned by Count Anton Grassalkovich who was the chair of the Royal Hungarian Chamber. Designed by F. A. Hillebrandt as a summer residence with a large French garden, it was built in 1760. In the past, the palace was famous as the hub of social life for the rich. Balls for aristocrats were held here with Joseph Haydn conducting Prince Eszterházy's court orchestra (See pp. 64 and 65).Today the palace is the Office of the Slovak President and it opens its doors to the public once a year on a Saturday in the middle of June. The garden serves the public all the year round. (See pp. 48 and 49). 🔍 2 CS 11

6 Reduta

Close to the bank of the Danube on the site of an old granary, Reduta was built in an eclectic style in 1913-1919. It is one of Bratislava's most elegant buildings. It housed one of the first cinemas, balls were held here and concerts performed. Currently, it is the seat of the Slovak Philharmonic and concerts are performed in the spacious concert hall with its 700 seat capacity. (See pp. 62 and 63). Anyone wishing to experience a traditional ball should certainly not miss the Bratislava Ball which takes place in Reduta in January and is the high point of the ball season. (See pp. 58 and 59). 🔍 2 CV 29

7 Academia Istropolitana

The first university within the territory of present-day Slovakia was founded by King Matthias Corvinus with the name of Academia Istropolitana in 1465. Of the original complex of buildings, only a part has survived on Ventúrska street around a large courtyard. Famous European scholars, among them the famed German astronomer, Johann Müller Regiomontanus, gave lectures at this university. 🔍 2 CQ 26

8 City Fortifications

The city fortifications were erected in the 14th century and consisted of high stone castle walls, another wall half the height of the former in front of them and a moat. The walls were reinforced by bastions. The city could be entered through three main gates and a fourth smaller one led out to the Danube. In the course of subsequent developments, the greater part of the fortifications was demolished in the 18th century. Only St. Michael's Gate (see pp. 34 and 35) has survived and the stretch of wall approximately 200 metres long by St. Martin's Cathedral. 🔍 2 CO 26

9 Mirbach Palace

Between 1768 and 1770, a brewery owner commissioned the town's most beautiful Rococo palace, designed by Franz Anton Hillebrandt. Its last owner, Count Mirbach, bequeathed it to the town to establish a gallery there. The courtyard of the palace contains a fountain by Viktor Tilgner. Since the palace is built on an irregular plot of land, the architect designed two portals in order to maintain the palace's symmetry; the one on the right is a blank. The palace houses the Bratislava City Gallery and displays of Baroque art are exhibited there. 🔍 2 CT 21

10 Aspremont Palace

The summer palace of Count Aspremont was designed by Johann Thalherr in 1769, outside the city walls. Later it was owned by Prince Eszterházy, whose court conductor was Joseph Haydn. The main façade of the palace gives onto the garden, originally in the French style, while the façade overlooking the street is simple and inconspicuous. Nowadays, the palace is the property of Comenius University. A large Medical Garden forms a part of the palace complex; the garden is open to the public and is an oasis of greenery and tranquillity in the busy city centre. (See pp. 48 and 49). 🔍 2 DL 7

🎵 Concerts in Mirbach Palace

"Sunday Matinée" concerts of classical music are held in Mirbach Palace at 10.30 every Sunday except for July and August.

Churches and Synagogues

1 Blue Church

St. Elizabeth's Church, also called the "Blue Church" on account of its colour, was built in the period 1910-1913. It was designed by the Budapest architect Edmund Lechner in the Hungarian Art Nouveau style with some oriental features. It is remark-

able for the fine detailed work on its façade with the frequent use of mosaic decoration. Many visitors regard this little gem as the most beautiful church in Bratislava and the fact that marriage and christening services in the church are booked far in advance is an indicator of its popularity with the locals. 🔲 2 DG 24

2 Trinitarian Church

The church and monastery were finished in 1727 close behind the fortification walls. The church is thought originally to have had two roofs in the High Baroque style which were probably destroyed in the French bombardment of 1809. St. Peter's Church in Vienna, which belongs to the same order, served as the model for the Trinitarian Church, the interior of which is the most complete and best-preserved in Bratislava. A large cupola with a trompe l'œil fresco painted by Antonio Galli Bibiena, a member of a famous Italian family of theatre decorative painters, dominates the roof-space. 🔲 2 CR 18

3 Great Lutheran Church

There have long been two Lutheran churches in the town – a larger one for German Lutherans and a smaller one for Slovaks and Hungarians. In 1774-76 a new church was built which was used by German worshippers. In 1778, in close proximity to this church, a smaller one was built for the Slovak and Hungarian faithful. As was dictated by tradition, the exteriors and interiors of both are simple. They also have no tower and the main entrance

does not give onto a square. 🔲 2 CO 15

4 St. Elizabeth's Church

The church and hospital were built to a design by Franz Anton Pilgram in 1739-43. Although the church has several times suffered damage, it has each time been restored to its original appearance with care and sensitivity. It is one of the best -preserved churches in Bratislava. The fresco and altar paintings were painted by Paul Troger and the statues embellishing the church were by Ludwig Gode, a student of Georg Raphael Donner. 🔲 2 DD 17

5 Merciful Brothers

The complex of the Merciful Brothers, comprising a church, monastery and hospital, was built just behind the town walls at the end of the 17th century, and was modelled on a Viennese monastery. The complex of buildings dominates the whole square which, because of the markets held here in the 18th and 19th centuries, was the busiest square in the town. The interior of the church dates back to the 18th century. In the past, the hospital played

an important role during periods of war and epidemics. 🔲 2 CX 18

6 St. Catherine's Chapel

The chapel was established by the Order of Cistercians, which owned the neighbouring house, in 1311. Although its architecture is simple, the chapel is one of the oldest remaining Gothic structures in the city. Its current façade dates back to the middle of the 19th century. The chapel is a real island of peace and tranquillity in the otherwise busy Michalská street. 🔲 2 CR 21

🎵 Music in churches

The tradition of high-quality music in churches continues today. Many churches hold regular choral performances, e.g.:

Franciscan Church – *every Wednesday at 7:30 p.m. Performances by various youth religious choirs*

Jesuit Church – *on Mondays at 8 p.m. from October to June; performance by university choirs*
Trinitarian Church – *on Sundays at 9 a.m.; performance by a religious choir*

7 Church and Convent of the Clare Nuns

Building work on the church and convent of the Clare Nuns started at the end of the 13th century and finished at the end of the 14th century. The unusual pentagonal church tower was built around 1400. It is one of the most highly regarded masterpieces of Gothic architecture in the city. In 1640 Giacomo and Giovanni Rava completed their reconstruction of the convent in the late Renaissance style. The church closed in 1782 and then served as home for various schools. The famous Hungarian composers, Ernest von Dohnányi and Béla Bartók (see p. 64), attended classes here. Today, concerts are held in the church, and the former convent building is an integral part of the University Library. 🔲 2 CP 22

coco pulpit by Ludwig Gode in 1753 is worthy of your attention. The pulpit is regarded as one of the most beautiful in Slovakia. 🔲 2 CT 22

9 Synagogue

There is a reference to Jews as already being inhabitants when Bratislava received its charter of municipal rights in 1291. The Jewish community in Bratislava was one of the longest established and most important in the whole of the Hungarian Kingdom. Until the Second World War, Jews made up approximately 10 % of Bratislava's inhabitants. Of the original three synagogues, only the one in Heydukova street has survived. This remarkable building was built in 1923-26 to a design by Artur Szalatnai-Slatinský. It is distinguished by its Ecclesiastical features and Cubist details. 🔲 2 CZ 17

> ℹ️ Visits must be arranged in advance:
> 📠 fax +421 2 5441 6949 @ memorial@znoba.sk

10 Church of the Ursuline Nuns

The church of the Ursuline Nuns was built in 1659 as a small Lutheran church for the Slovak and Hungarian faithful. After its confiscation in 1672, it was assigned to the Ursuline Nuns. Shortly afterwards, the tower was added and in 1687 also the convent and school.
This relatively small church is distinguished for its authentically elegant Baroque style in the interior. 🔲 2 CV 20

8 Jesuit church

The church was built in 1638 as a large Lutheran church for the German faithful. By the king's decree, it was required to differ from Catholic churches. It was not allowed to have either tower, presbytery or its main entrance from a square. However, despite this decree, the main entrance was so constructed. In 1672 the church was confiscated from the Lutherans and assigned to the Jesuits. They altered the interior but the simple protestant architecture was retained. The Ro-

Courtyards and Cellars

1 Apponyi Palace

Once inside the gateway, an old cart with a wine cask catches your eye. The relatively small courtyard is dominated by two large wine presses surrounded by a number of old wooden tables and benches belonging to the Café Apponyi. This place exudes an atmosphere of history in a way unlike any other. In the gateway, there is the entrance to the Museum of Viticulture, part of which is housed in the Mediaeval cellars. 🔲 2 CU 24

2 The Old Town Hall

The Old Town Hall courtyard is one of the few readily discovered by tourists themselves. (See pp. 28 and 29). It is one of the architecturally best -preserved and it possesses excellent acoustics.

For this reason, the courtyard is the venue for concerts and theatre performances, as well as craft fairs and wine-tastings. Access to the Bratislava City Museum is from this courtyard. (See pp. 60 and 61). 🔲 2 CU 23

3 The Primate's Palace

The elegant courtyard of the Primate's Palace should not escape the attention of any visitor to the palace. The centre of the courtyard is dominated by the Fountain of St. George from the 17th century which pre-dates the palace by more than a hundred years. In summer grand re-

ceptions are held here. The entrance to the palace's chapel is located in the corner of the courtyard. (See pp. 22-25). The courtyard is joined to another courtyard with a complex of statues of St. John Nepomuck. Following on in this way, you enter the romantic courtyard of the Ruttkay Palace. 🔲 2 CV 23

4 Ruttkay Palace

On stepping into this courtyard of the Renaissance house with arcades from the 16th century, you feel as though touched by a soft Mediterranean breeze. The palace is accessible from the gate in Uršulínska street or through the court-

yard of the Primate's Palace on working days up to 5 p.m.

The fountain with four urinating boys stands in the courtyard. (See pp. 26 and 47). 🔲 2 CX 23

5 Čierny Havran (Black Raven)

At the entrance to Biela street, a signboard and, in the evening, torches invite you to enter the courtyard of this Renaissance house from the 16th century. This welcoming courtyard with Renaissance arcades is used by a popular restaurant on the ground floor of the house. Thanks to its romantic atmosphere, the courtyard is fully occupied during warm summer evenings. The cellar houses a small theatre. 🔍 2 CS 22

6 Segner House

This Renaissance house of a type not typical of this region was built on Michalská street in 1648. A famous mathematician and physician, Johann Andreas von Segner was born here in 1707. Although the courtyard of the house is more a long passageway than a typical courtyard of the period, it is one of the most interesting in the city, now accommodating a number of small fashion shops and galleries. In the quaint cellars, pubs and restaurants are located. 🔍 2 CR 21

7 Jeszenák Palace

The palace was built in 1730 and is one of the oldest Baroque palaces in the city. The courtyard houses a small gallery displaying the works of well-known Slovak artists and distinctive Bratislava antiques. You can have a cup of tea in the tea-shop while visiting the famous gallery in the beautiful cellar. 🔍 2 CT 21

8 House No. 7

This Renaissance house in Ventúrska street, originally from the 17th century, which has recently been reconstructed, is a good example of the harmonisation of past and present architecture. Its glass-roofed court-

yard is among the most stylish in Bratislava. The main part, beyond the preserved Mediaeval well, is occupied by small fashion shops and a modern restaurant. 🔍 2 CR 25

9 Zichy Palace

The Palace of Count Zichy was built in 1775. From 1817 to 1820 the German composer, Heinrich Marschner, was music teacher to the Zichy family. (See pp. 64-65). The courtyard, typical of the late 18th century, has a modern fountain in its centre. The palace is the property of the city of Bratislava and weddings are performed on the first floor. On Saturdays, it is interesting to watch married couples in the courtyard. In summer, the courtyard serves as a public reading place and, due to its excellent acoustics, jazz concerts are given here. 🔍 2 CR 22

10 House No.12

It is simply the beautiful passageway with decorations in the Renaissance and Gothic styles and the wooden cobbles forming the pavement into house No.12 on Michalská street which entice you further into the courtyard. Following an exhaustive reconstruction, another delightful corner bringing with it the southern atmosphere reminiscent of the old Pressburg has appeared in the city. Well-known shops and also an attractive bar and a small antiques shop are to be found here. 🔍 2 CR 21

🏛 Cellars and Courtyards

A great number of courtyards and cellars in Bratislava relate to the viticulture tradition of the city. They are the most characteristic features of the historical centre of the city. In Mediaeval times, the lives of the majority of residents were bound up with wine production and the wine trade. Presses stood in the courtyards of the houses and wine was produced in the cellars. Even today, a lot of the houses in the Old Town still have former wine cellars and courtyards. A number of restaurants, bars, pubs, as well as small theatres, are to be found in these cellars. In romantic courtyards you often find antiques shops, galleries or cafes. If you want to get under the skin of Bratislava, you need to be provided with plenty of curiosity. You won't regret it.

Fountains

1 Ganymede Fountain

One of the most famous and elegant fountains in Bratislava is sited directly in front of the Opera House. It was constructed at the same time as the Opera House (1888) and was a gift to the city from an important Bratislava bank. It depicts the story from the Greek myths of Ganymede, a young boy who was abducted by Zeus in the shape of an eagle. (See p. 32). ▣ 2 CV 26

2 Fountain of Friendship

What is undoubtedly the biggest fountain in Bratislava stands in the large square in front of the Office of the Slovak Government. Completed in 1980, the giant fountain depicts a flower of 9 metres in diameter, from which water sprays and cascades over the large steps around it. Students from the nearby university relax in the surrounding park. ▣ 2 CZ 5

3 Duck Fountain

The square in which the fountain is placed was designed in its current form at the turn of the 19th-20th centuries. A new quarter was established here following the construction of the Old Bridge. The park was planted in the centre of the square in 1900, having at its heart a beautiful fountain composed of statues of boys catching ducks, designed in 1914 by a well-known master, Robert Kühmayer. The park is a pocket of calm in the middle of one of the busiest squares in Bratislava. ▣ 2 DF 27

4 Birds' Fountain

This unusual fountain stands at the junction of two important streets in the Old Town. It is a replica of a fountain cast in 1900. Originally, there were several fountains like this in Bratislava. What makes it interesting is the fact that it is made up of three tiers, the upper of which was intended for birds, the middle for people and the lower for horses. ▣ 2 CQ 26

5 Moat

Following a major reconstruction, in 2002 Hviezdoslav's Square again became a popular pedestrian promenade. The promenade is lined by a 70 metre-long fountain recalling the moat which was to be found here up to the 18th century. In summer, the water flowing in the fountain refreshes the air and indicates the time – the water jets increase in height every hour. (See p. 48). ▣ 2 CS 28

6 Maximilian Fountain

The oldest of Bratislava's fountains stands in the Main Square (Hlavné námestie). It was built in 1572 and is topped by the figure of Maximilian II in knight's armour. In 1563 he became the first king to be crowned in Bratislava, and presented the fountain to the town after a devastating fire. The central part was originally decorated with statues of urinating boys; these were replaced in the 18th century by statues of boys with dolphins. (See pp. 26 and 44). ▣ 2 CT 24

7 Urinating Boys

In the courtyard of Ruttkay Palace you can find what is probably the most entertaining fountain in the whole city. Although it matches the surrounding Renaissance -style courtyard, the fountain did not stand here originally. The main part of the fountain is composed of four naked urinating boys two of whom are holding hands. These statues were removed from their original position in the central part of Maximilian's Fountain. They were found by chance during demolition works of quarters below the Castle (See pp. 26 and 44). 🔲 2 CX 23

8 St. George's Fountain

The fountain in the Primate's Palace courtyard dates back to the middle of the 17th century and depicts St. George slaying the dragon. It is one of the most highly regarded and originally stood in the unique Italian-style botanical garden attached to what was formerly the Archbishop's summer residence. (See p. 40). The fountain was only installed in the courtyard at the beginning of the 20th century. 🔲 2 CV 23

9 A Woman with a Jug

This has stood in the centre of the Franciscan Square since the 16th century. As only its basin survived, an allegory of a woman with a jug was installed in the centre of the fountain from 1804. In the past the fountain was used by firemen as a water source. 🔲 2 CT 22

10 Fountain of Peace

The fountain depicting the globe with doves was built in 1980 in front of the Grassalkovich Palace. It is a popular meeting place for friends and lovers before setting off for the delights of the city centre and it is also a place to relax in the centre of a busy city. 🔲 2 CS 12

Parks, gardens, historical cemeteries

1 Hill Park

The Hill Park (Horský park) can be regarded as the green lungs of Bratislava. There are probably not many European cities which have a patch of woodland right in the centre of the city. From 1869, this area of protected

natural woodland was gradually transformed into a public park. In 1892, the park was further enlarged and a network of paths, benches and streams was created. The park remains very popular today; people come here for walking, jogging, cycling or to take their children to visit a foresters' house with animals. ◳ 1 AM 11

2 St. Andrew's Cemetery

This park-like cemetery (Ondrejský cintorín) is one of the oldest in Bratislava. It was established in 1784 in the fields surrounding the Aspremont Palace. A number of important people from Bratislava's past are buried here. Although some precious tombs and family vaults have not survived, there are still many richly decorated tombstones. The cemetery is a quiet green oasis in the centre of a bustling city. ◳ 2 DM 14

3 Goat's Gate Cemetery

The Lutheran cemetery at Goat's Gate (Cintorín pri Kozej bráne) was founded in 1783. At that time it was located on the periphery of the

city, surrounded by meadows and vineyards. It was gradually extended and more greenery planted. In the tombs and vaults of high artis-

tic and architectural quality, many prominent citizens are buried. It is the best-preserved cemetery in Bratislava and thanks to its romantic atmosphere and rich greenery undoubtedly worth the short walk. ◳ 2 CG 13

4 Janko Kráľ Park

Just a 15-minute walk away from the Old Town, Bratislava's second largest park extends over what were formerly floodplain forests on the right bank of the Danube. It was founded in 1775-1776 and is one of the oldest public parks in Europe. The original French-style park was transformed into a landscaped park in the English style in 1832. At the end of the 19th century, the original Gothic tower of the Franciscan Church was transferred to the park (See pp. 30-31). It is frequently visited by Bratislavans looking for somewhere to rest or to play sports. ◳ 1 AV 32

5 Garden of Grassalkovich Palace

Following the reconstruction in 1999, which restored the garden to its original shape, it is now the most beautiful garden in Bratislava. It was established along with the palace in 1760 as a French-style garden. Although the palace is the Office of the Slovak President, the garden is open to the public. Various modern art-forms and sculptures are displayed here. Thanks to its attraction and central location, the garden is a favourite place for local people and tourists to relax. ◳ 2 CT 9

6 Medical Garden

The garden surrounding the Aspremont Palace was established in 1769 at the same time as the Palace itself. The garden in the French style was set out close to the palace; at the rear was planted a fruit orchard, the entrance lined with a thick row of trees. After the First World War, the palace became a part of the Faculty of Medicine, which gave the garden its name – Medical. It is popular with students of medicine as well as with children for whom a playground was constructed at the back of the garden. A memorial to the famous Hungarian poet, Sándor Petöfi, is also sited in this garden. 🔍 2 DK 10

7 Hviezdoslavovo Square

The site of what is now the park in Hviezdoslavovo square was occupied up to 1775 by a moat. The area formed after the moat was filled in became a promenade with avenues of plane trees and a popular place to stroll. In the further part of the park was built an arbour in which concerts are held in summer. In the central part, a large

play out their contests with big wooden chessmen. 🔍 2 CS 28

8 City Moat

The last vestige of the moat which once surrounded the city walls is to be seen at St. Michael's Gate. In periods of peace, shooting competitions were held here and in the 18th century theatrical performances. The ditch is a strip of greenery right in the centre of the Old Town and, following its reconstruction, has become yet another romantic niche in Bratislava. 🔍 2 CR 19

9 Liszt Garden

Liszt Garden is the sole example of a palace garden within the former town walls. It belongs to the complex of the De Pauli Palace built in 1776. At the end of a small garden is a Rococo pavilion in which the young Franz Liszt gave his first public concert in 1820. Ac-

cess to the garden is from the palace or from Klariská street. There is also a small amphitheatre where concerts are held. (See pp. 40 and 64). 🔍 2 CQ 24

10 Botanical Gardens

The Botanical Gardens of Comenius University were founded in 1942 in close proximity to the Danube. Over the decades, more than 10,000 plant species from all over the world have been planted over an area of 6.5 hectares. The most attractive parts are a large rose-garden in the centre, the part dedicated to succulent plants, and the various greenhouses, each devoted to a different temperature zone. The season most recommended for a visit is April-May when many flowers are in bloom. 🔍 1 AA 21

> ℹ️ Opening hours: 1st April – 30th October

chessboard is laid out where amateur chess players, with encouragement from bystanders,

Statues and Memorials

1 Franz Liszt

The bust of the famous composer who began his career in Bratislava and was a frequent visitor to the city, is sited in a small square in front of St. Martin's Cathedral to the right of the steps. It was created in 1911 by a famous Bratislava sculptor,

Victor Tilgner, who was based in Vienna. The wrought-iron railing in the form of notes is of special interest. (See pp. 40 and 41, 64 and 65). 🔍 2 CP 27

2 Watcher (Čumil)

Paradoxically, what is undoubtedly the most often-photographed statue does not actually depict anyone in particular. Since 1997, the bronze figure of a smiling man emerging from a drain inspection-cover has adorned the most visited place in the pedestrian zone, where probably every visitor to Bratislava will walk at least once. It didn't take long for people to make up a number of jokes and stories about Čumil. Which was precisely the intention of the figure's creator, Viktor Hulík. 🔍 2 CU 25

3 Chatam Sofer Memorial

The memorial to the famous Jewish rabbi is situated near the Danube. The architecturally remarkable construction is built over the remains

of the orthodox Jewish cemetery which was used between 1670 and 1847. In addition to the grave of rabbi Chatam Sofer (1762-1839), another twenty-two graves of important members of the Jewish community are located here. Sofer's memorial is a pilgrimage site for orthodox Jews from all over the world. 🔍 1 AL 27

> ℹ️ Visits must be arranged in advance:
> ☎ fax +421 2 5441 6949
> @ memorial@znoba.sk

4 "Schöne Náci"

In an attempt to make the pedestrian zone more attractive, the city representatives commissioned famous artists to create sculptures recalling famous people from the past. "Schöne Náci", whose original name was Ignác, was a memorable Bratislava eccentric in the first half of the 20th century. He was a poor recluse who made a living from cleaning carpets. However, dressed in his old tail-coat, stovepipe hat and carrying a cane, he would stroll through the town, greeting people with his hat raised, and bowing to the ladies. Quite simply, he belonged to Bratislava and its people loved him. The statue was created by sculptor Juraj Meliš. 🔍 2 CU 25

5 St. Elizabeth

The statue of St. Elizabeth of Thuringia/Hungary (1207-1231) which was displayed in the Park of Bratislava Castle in 2000, commemorates the fact that she was born in 1207 in the Castle, a daughter of the Hungarian King Andrew II, and betrothed to be married at the age of four. She was made a saint in

1235 for her charitable works and the help she gave to the sick and the poor. 🔍 2 CK 26

6 Johann Nepomuk Hummel

The memorial to the Bratislava-born composer J. N. Hummel (1778-835) is a masterpiece by Viktor Tilgner and was first displayed in 1887. Up to 1904 the statue was located in the park in front of the Municipal Theatre, then moved to several other sites and eventually finished up in front of Nestor Palace, the residence of the German Embassy. (See pp. 61 and 64). 🔍 2 CR 29

9 Napoleonic Soldier

Directly in front of the French Embassy, the bronze statue by sculptor Juraj Meliš of a Napoleonic soldier leaning on a bench was installed in 1997. Tourists like having their photographs taken as his companion. As his hat sits deep on his nose and completely prevents him from seeing anything, he should humorously evoke that part of the city's history associated with Napoleon, who twice besieged the city. 🔍 2 CT 23

10 Georg Raphael Donner

On the square in front of St.

7 Pavol Ország-Hviezdoslav

The memorial statue to one of the most important Slovak poets and writers was positioned in 1937 on the square in front of the Slovak National Theatre. This large statue depicts Hviezdoslav (1849-1921) seated, composing a poem. 🔍 2 CT 27

8 Sándor Petöfi

This memorial to the famous Hungarian poet Sándor Petöfi (1823-1849) was unveiled in 1911 in the presence of Arch-duke Friederich in the park in front of the Municipal Theatre. It also has stood in a number of places and is currently situated in the Medical Garden. (See pp. 48 and 49). 🔍 2 DL 9

Martin's Cathedral to the left to the steps, the bust of the most famous Austrian Baroque sculptor, George Raphael Donner, has stood since 1883. He spent some of his life in Bratislava and took part in the reconstruction of the Cathedral in the Baroque style. (See pp.18 and 19). 🔍 2 CP 28

Modernist Buildings

1 Baťa Store

This store, built in 1929-1930 for the footwear manufacturer Baťa, was designed by his "court"-exclusive architect Vladimír Karfík who worked for Le Corbusier and later in the studio of Frank Lloyd Wright. In its time it was a very progressive building reminiscent of the German Bauhaus style. 🔍 2 CS 19

2 Municipal Savings

This building was erected

between 1927 and 1931 and was one of the first in Slovakia with distinctively modern architectural features. The new materials used in its façade were unique at that time and made this building the most progressive in the city for a long time to come. 🔍 2 DB 22

3 Department Store

One of the first stores in Slovakia, this was built in 1928-1929 on the elegant Štefánikova street which dates from the turn of the century. Being adjacent to richly-decorated houses constructed in imitation of various architectural styles, at the time it probably affronted passersby. The store is a typical example of the Bauhaus style. 🔍 2 CX 20

4 House No. 7

This high-quality house was constructed on Hviezdoslavovo square in 1935 to a design by the Czech architect Bohuslav

Fuchs. This house, with an appearance which even today still looks modern, is characterised by its plastically protruding balconies which give the façade a dynamic look. 🔍 2 CS 28

5 Manderla House

This, the first tall building in Bratislava, was designed by the architects Ludwig and Spitzer. It was erected in the period 1933-1935 in the face of a storm of protests and even now it causes problems for traffic as it sticks out into a busy junction. However, it has become an integral part of the city panorama. 🔍 2 DA 21

6 Houses of Cooperative Associations

A complex of high-standard administrative buildings of similar pat-

tern, designed by Emil Belluš and constructed in succession between 1934-1939. Each has a passage with shops on the ground-floor and offices and flats on the upper floors. 🔍 2 DA 20

7 Brouk Store

This store, which was built in 1935 in the unbelievably short period of 90 days, was designed by Christian Ludwig on a relatively small plot of land. Its character was based on rules adopted from the designs of American stores. The shop windows are of exceptional interest. 🔍 2 CX 20

8 Blocks of flats Avion

A complex of flats dating from 1930-31 is an example of a new approach to living. The "Purist-style" architecture is expressed in the rectangular structures separated by loggias. The house was built in eleven months. 🔍 2 DH 8

9 Luxor House

This multi-functional building with a simple façade, which dominates one of the busiest streets in Bratislava, was built in 1937-39. The lower floors were designed for shops, restaurants and offices

and the upper floors for flats. 🔍 2 DB 23

10 Villa Dr. Dvořák

The house was built in the villa area near the Castle in 1933 and is one of the best examples of Le Corbusier-influenced architecture in Slovakia. The progressive character of the villa represented a new concept of living in the thirties. 🔍 2 CA 21

Buildings of Socialism

1 Petržalka

The right bank of the Danube was originally inhabited by about 30,000 residents living in family houses. In 1973, the decision was taken for the demolition of the greater part of the original Petržalka. As early as 1976 the first people moved into the new concrete blocks of flats. In the course of the next ten years, the largest area of blocks of flats in the country was erected here and became home to 125,000 inhabitants. Petržalka is not a ghetto but neither does it offer luxury living. It is mostly inhabited by younger people and it has the highest proportion of university graduates in Slovakia.

2 New Bridge

The New Bridge was constructed in 1967-72 as the second bridge in Bratislava. This indisputably technically interesting and unique work met with a positive response from the community of architects; however, the residents reacted negatively. Despite the protests, hundreds of historical buildings were demolished in the course of the construction work. The steel suspension construction is complemented by a sloping pylon with a panoramic restaurant at a height of 80 metres. Regardless of the controversy it provoked, the bridge was declared the Building of the Century in Slovakia. 🔍 2 CO 31

3 TV Tower

The TV Tower which was built in 1968-73 on the Kamzík hill above Bratislava is an inherent dominant feature of the city. Thanks to its height of nearly 200 m, it is visible from a considerable distance. At a height of 80 m there is a panoramic-view rotating restaurant. Without leaving your seat or table, you can survey the whole of Bratislava and, in the right weather conditions, even Vienna. 🔍 3 FG 5

4 Radio Building

Due to its colour, size and illogical shape, the radio building which was built in 1971-84 is one of the prominent features of the city. It is a massive steel construction in the shape of an inverted pyramid concealed under which is a concert hall with the capacity for 600 visitors. 🔍 1 BA 15

5 Freedom Square

Originally just a large plot of land in front of the Archbishop's Summer Palace (see pp.40 and 41), this was only developed after the Second World War. The centre of the square is dominated by a giant fountain with cascades from 1978-80 (see pp. 46 and 47). The western part of this large square is bounded by the first building of today's Slovak Technical University (STU) from 1947-51 which in its style and quality echoes the architecture of the pre-war period. The eastern side is occu-

pied by the building of the then Post Palace built between 1946-51, representative of the best of the pre-war traditions. On the south side of the square stands another building of the STU, built in 1958-62. 🔍 2 CZ 5

6 Blocks of Flats Februárka

A huge shortage of flats and an attempt to accelerate building work and create cheaper flats resulted in the invention of new building technologies. The first construction of con-

crete blocks of flats in Slovakia, near Račianske mýto, was started in 1956. The housing complex is designed as detached blocks with shops and services on the ground-floor. The houses were built using the new technology of poured concrete. 🔲 1 BC 11

7 Mladá Garda Hostel

The architecture dating from the period 1950-55 can be characterised as an attempt to create a

new style combining historical styles and folk art. The most prominent example of socialist realism in Bratislava is the hostel for undergraduates Mladá Garda situated in Račianska ulica which was built between 1954-56 to a design by the architect Emil Belluš. The complex, providing accommodation for 2,500 students, is decorated with Renaissance-style ornamentation. 🔲 3 FJ 5

8 Slavín

The largest war memorial in Central Europe was erected in 1957-60. It is located on one of the most prominent sites in Bratislava in the middle of the most exclusive villa quarter on one of the hills above the city. Thanks to its position and its height of 52 m, it is one of the dominant features of the city. Nearly 7,000 soldiers of the Red Army who lost their lives in the battles at the end of War World II are buried in the cemetery surrounding the memorial. The memorial offers a panoramic view of a great part of the city. 🔲 2 CH 2

9 Prior Store

The biggest department store in the centre of Bratislava comprises two inter-connected buildings. The older building was built in 1964-68 and the later one in 1972-78. Along with the tall building of the Kiev Hotel attached to the store, they form a distinctive feature in the centre of the city. In order to construct them, an entire block of buildings from earlier periods had to be demolished. 🔲 2 DC 21

10 Slovak National Gallery

The modern extension to the Slovak National Gallery dating from 1969-77 is one of the most controversial and contentious buildings in the city. Its aggressive and dynamic architecture contrasts sharply with the neighbouring buildings. 🔲 2 CU 31

🏛 A View of the City

The most spectacular bird's eye view of the city is from the viewing platform on the New Bridge at a height of 95 m. You'll feel as though you could reach out and touch the Castle. One floor below is the attractive café and restaurant UFO. ➥ *u-f-o.sk*

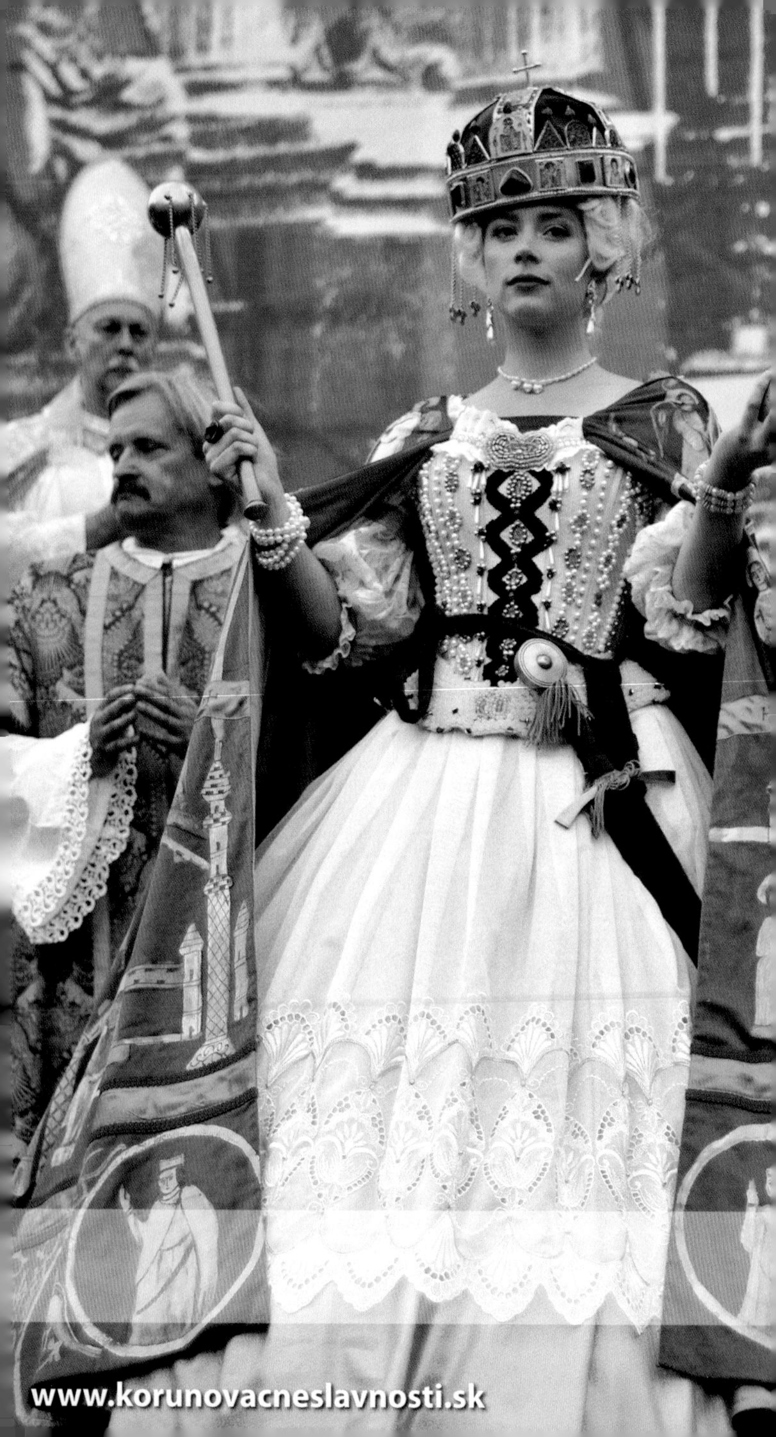
www.korunovacneslavnosti.sk

Cultural Events & Leisure

Celebrations and Festivals

1 Season of Balls

Like neighbouring Vienna, Bratislava also has its long tradition of balls. In the course of the carnival season, the whole social whirl focuses around

balls, though it's hard to count exactly how many are held in Bratislava. As a rule, the grandest of all the balls are held each year in the most imposing buildings – in Reduta and in the Opera House. The carnival season in Bratislava is quite simply an event marked by waltzes and elegant gowns.

⤷ visit.bratislava.sk

2 Flamenco Festival

At the end of November every year, the Flamenco Festival is held in Bratislava, with the aim of popularising this Andalusian art. The festival is a showcase for the best music and dance groups, Flamenco soloists from Andalusia and Slovakia as well as courses and workshops for Flamenco.

⤷ flamenco.sk

3 Bratislava in Motion Festival

This international festival dedicated to contemporary dance is held every year in Bratislava in June. During the course of its two weeks, well-known groups of dancers from all over the world put on contemporary performances. The festival is the big-

gest of its kind in Slovakia and during this period Bratislava lives the life of modern dance.

⤷ abp.sk

4 Cultural Summer

From mid June to mid September, the streets, squares, churches and courtyards of the Old Town become the venues where the Cultural Summer performances are given. This, the longest-lasting of Bratislava's festivals, more than compensates in its variety for the closure of the theatres and concert halls in July and August. Concerts of various kinds, theatre performances, exhibitions, craft markets, performances of folk groups and a number of other cultural events transform the outdoors of the Old Town into one big stage.

⤷ visit.bratislava.sk

5 Coronation Ceremonies

Another event that attracts a number of foreign and Slovak visitors is the Coronation Ceremony which is

held annually on the last weekend in June. Each year, a different one of the nineteen original coronation ceremonies is performed in St. Martin's Cathedral. Two hundred actors dressed in period costumes, a hundred and fifty craftsmen, an authentic replica of the religious service in the cathedral, a long procession through the city, ox roasting and jousting tournaments, all accompanied by a variety of historical music and dance make it a spectacular performance worth experiencing. (See pp 68-69).

⤷ korunovacneslavnosti.sk

6 Old Craftsmen's Days

Regularly, at the beginning of September, the heart of the Old Town changes into a craftsmen's market as it would have looked a hundred years ago. Craftsmen and masters of folk arts from all over the country demonstrate their skills in a display of their masterpieces and traditions which are still alive in Slovakia. Potters, smiths, woodcarvers, embroidery-makers, producers of musical instruments, bells and others fill the square and courtyards echoing with talk and folk music. You can taste local wines and traditional specialities and you can have a go at producing something by your own hand.

7 Bratislava Music Festival

The Bratislava Music Festival (BHS) is the greatest and the best-known festival of classical music in Slovakia.

Ever since 1964, this exceptional event has been organised every year in autumn. In the course of two weeks, Bratislava experiences the peak of the musical season represented by the many performances by famous artists and musical bodies that are held in various venues around the city.

bhsfestival.sk

8 Viva Musica!

Every June / July, for ten days, the heart of the Old Town – Hviezdoslav's square is transformed into a huge summer amphitheatre to house the biggest summer festival of classical music in Bratis-

lava with a large number of artists, concerts of classical music, and also children's opera. This modern festival of classical music introduces the most talented stars of the young generation of classical music and also introduces Bratislava as a European cultural destination, where young esprit, rich tradition and the dynamics of the modern time intermingle.

vivamusica.sk

9 Bratislava Jazz Days

Every year, this well-established festival, organised in the second half of October, attracts a large number of jazz fans to Bratislava. Back in 1975 when a group of enthusiasts started the festival, no one could have expected that it would develop into one of the most famous festivals in Europe with regular concerts given by the world's biggest names in jazz.

bjd.sk

10 Christmas Market

The Friday before the first Sunday in Advent is the opening date for the traditional Christmas Market on the Main Square, an event extremely popular with both residents of Bratislava and visitors alike. The large variety of goods on offer has one common theme – only those products associated with Christmas are sold here. Despite the cold, Bratislavans meet here after work and chat through the evening with their friends over a glass or two of mulled wine. 2 CT 24

visit.bratislava.sk

Galleries and Museums

1 Slovak National Gallery

The Slovak National Gallery (SNG) is the biggest and the most important of the galleries in Slovakia. It consists of a complex of buildings on the banks of the Danube. The core of its activity is Slovak art; however, an integral part of the collection of the SNG comprises art of European provenance. Amongst the major exhibitions are Gothic Art in Slovakia, Baroque Art in Slovakia, Slovak Painting of the 19th century and European Painting from the 16th to the 19th centuries. 2 CU 31

sng.sk

2 Bratislava City Gallery

After the Slovak National Gallery, the Bratislava City Gallery is the second largest and most important gallery in Slovakia. It is focused on exhibiting its extensive collection of paintings and regularly presents Slovak and worldwide fine arts from the Gothic period up to the most up-to-date trends. Mirbach Palace houses the permanent exhibition of Central European Baroque fine arts, while in Pálffy Palace can be seen the permanent exhibition of Gothic panel paintings and plastic arts, Central European fine

arts of the 19th century and fine arts of the 20th century in Slovakia. 2 CR 26

gmb.sk

3 Bratislava City Museum

The exhibition of the Bratislava City Museum in the Old Town Hall provides an approach to the history of the city from the Mediæval period up to the 20th century. The history of crafts and trade, coronations of the Kings of the Hungarian Kingdom, cultural life of the city, sacred art, the life-style of aristocrats and burghers, the ideas of the national enlightenment as well as the achievements of the industrial development in the second half of the 19th and the beginning of the 20th centuries are all on display here. 2 CU 23

muzeum.bratislava.sk

4 The Treasury of the Museum of Archaeology

The Treasury is located in Bratislava Castle and displays the most precious archaeological artefacts found in Slovakia dating from the Late Stone Age up to the 13th century. The most precious artefact is the Venus of Moravany – a tiny but beautiful woman-like statue made from mammoth tusk about 22,800 years ago and found in the western Slovak village of Moravany. 2 CH 27

snm.sk

5 Danubiana – Meulensteen Art Museum

Danubiana was established in the magical year of 2000, symbolically on the banks of the Danube where three Central European countries – Slovakia, Austria and Hungary – meet. This architecturally attractive building shaped like a Roman galley is located on a narrow peninsula in the Danube just 15 km south of the city centre. The role of this newest museum of modern art in Bratislava is to present the most influential and remarkable representatives of Slovak and international fine art of the 20th century.

danubiana.sk

6 Museum of Transport

The Museum of Transport occupies a part of Bratislava's first Railway Station. In several halls and outside, this very interesting museum provides a display of road and rail transport from their beginnings up to the sixties and seventies of the twentieth century. Historical motorcycles, steam engines and official vehicles used by representatives of the socialist government are also on display. 🔍 1 AT 15

✑ muzeumdopravy.com

7 Museum of Jewish Culture

This museum provides information on the history and culture of Jews living in Slovakia who settled here around the 9th century. The exhibits show the daily life of the Jewish community, Jewish holidays, the interior of a Jewish synagogue and important people of Jewish origin who contributed to the fame of Slovakia. The final part of the exhibition commemorates the approximately 70, 000 Slovak Jews who were victims of the Holocaust. A visitor can learn about the life-cycle of a Jew from his birth to his death. 🔍 2 CM 22

✑ slovak-jewish-heritage.org

8 History Museum

The Museum of History which is housed in Bratislava Castle forms an important part of the Slovak National Museum. It documents the development of society in Slovakia from the Mediæval period up to the present day. The spacious exhibition halls situated on the 3rd floor of the Castle give visitors an insight into the interiors of the

houses of aristocracy and burghers within the Slovak territory during the period from the 16th up to the 20th century. A collection documenting the development of clock-making from the end of the 17th up to the beginning of the 20th centuries forms a part of the exhibition. 🔍 2 CH 27

✑ snm.sk

9 Hummel House

A small museum displays the life and the work of the important composer Johann Nepomuk Hummel (1770 – 1837), a student of Mozart. In two rooms on the second floor, documents are exhibited relating to the life and work of the composer and the interior has been fitted out with furniture of the period. Some examples of the artist's extensive work, such as manuscripts and later editions of his masterpieces are shown here. Also, two spinets which were played by the master are on display. 🔍 2 CX 22

✑ muzeum.bratislava.sk

10 Clock Museum

The exhibits of the Bratislava City Museum in the narrow Rococo House of the Good Shepherd document the rich history of clock-making in Bratislava from the end of the 17th up to the end of the 19th centuries. A unique set of mobile sun dials from the 17th-18th centuries, a variety of table and wall-clocks, alarm clocks and examples of pocket watches are displayed here. The majority of the exhibits carry the signature of Bratislava master clockmakers. 🔍 2 CN 26

✑ muzeum.bratislava.sk

Theatres, Concerts and Cinemas

1 Slovak Philharmonic

The largest and most beautiful concert hall in Bratislava is located in Reduta near the Danube embankment. This elegant hall dating from the beginning of the 20th century has the ca-

pacity for 700 people and is predominantly used for the regular concerts of the most famous Slovak musical body – the Slovak Philharmonic Orchestra. Also, the major part of the Bratislava Music Festival (BHS) takes place in this hall. In the carnival season, the most spectacular balls are held here. 🔍 2 CV 29

🖱 filharm.sk

2 Opera and Ballet

The opera and ballet productions of the Slovak National Theatre are staged in two buildings – the historical one and the modern one. The high quality of the productions, a rich tradition and well-established artists are the chief attractions not only for locals but also for visitors from abroad, especially from Vienna. The extensive repertoire of well-known as well as less fa-

miliar masterpieces and, at certain times, up to six performances a week guarantees that lovers of opera and ballet will be rewarded in Bratislava. 🔍 2 CV 26, 1 BD 27

🖱 snd.sk

3 Klarisky Concert Hall

This former convent church of the Claire nuns today serves as a concert hall. Its excellent acoustics and cosy atmosphere make this 14th century Gothic church, situated in a picturesque part of the Old Town, feel as though created for the purpose and it is used frequently. Regular concerts of chamber and choral music as well as jazz and guitar concerts take place here. 🔍 2 CP 22

🖱 visit.bratislava.sk

4 Aréna Theatre

The Aréna Theatre is one of the city's theatres with the longest tradition. The building was constructed in 1828 in a park on the true-right bank of the Danube and acquired its current form in 1899. Aréna was famous for the numerous performances given by foreign theatre companies, e.g. regular performances by the Theater an der Wien. The famous Max Reinhardt began his artistic career in this theatre when as a young actor he played here for several seasons. Aréna today offers a broad spectrum of genres from plays for children to musicals. 🔍 1 AY 32

🖱 divadloarena.sk

5 Slovak Radio

The Slovak Radio building in the shape of an "inverted pyramid" conceals a large concert studio with a capacity for 600 visitors. The home of the Slovak Radio Symphony Orchestra is famous for concerts performed by well-established artists as well as regular organ recitals given by artists from abroad. 🔍 1 BA 15

🖱 slovakradio.sk

6 Nová Scéna Theatre

The Nová scéna was founded as a theatre of music and entertainment with comedies prevailing; later, operettas were included in the repertoire. In recent years, it has become the leading scene for musicals in Bratislava. In addition to a wide range of internationally-known musicals, a great number of successful Slovak and Czech musicals are performed here as well. 🔍 2 CY 10

🖱 nova-scena.sk

7 Mladosť Cinema

This cinema is one of the few small cinemas in the centre of the city which, due to its specialisation, has survived the invasion of the multi-

plex cinemas. This cinema is the only one in the Old Town that frequently houses various film festivals and which focuses mainly on the productions of European cinematography. As in other cinemas in Slovakia, the films are shown in the original language and provided with Slovak subtitles. 🔲 2CR 28

8 Cinema City Aupark

The biggest multiplex in Slovakia is to be found within the gigantic Aupark shopping centre which opened in 2002. The centre is situated on the true- right bank of the Danube next to the large historical park and is accessible on foot from the Old Town by bridge. 12 cinema halls fully equipped with the latest technology offer entertainment to an audience of more than 2300. Thanks to its capacity, the cinema is the venue for the well-known International Film Festival. 🔲 1 AT 35

🖙 cinemacity.sk

9 Cinema City Eurovea

The exclusive Palace Cinemas multiplex is situated on the bank of the River Danube in the newly-opened Eurovea international shopping centre. You can watch films on nine screens with a total capacity of 1,643 seats. All of the halls have special "double-seats" called Love seats, which are an exclusive new feature of Slovak cinemas. This means the city centre now boasts a modern

cinema multiplex and bar with VIP zone for special events.
Pribinova 8, 🔲 2 DL 29

🖙 cinemacity.sk

In the Steps of Music Composers

❸ Wolfgang Amadeus Mozart (1756-1791)

This musical genius visited the town just once, to give one of his first public concerts, at the age of six. This happened in 1762 when he accepted an invitation to play before the local aristocracy from Count Pálffy, who had heard of Mozart's exceptional talent. The young Wolfgang was accompanied from Vienna by his father. It was the only concert given by Mozart in the Hungarian Kingdom.

❶ Béla Bartók (1881-1945)

This, the greatest Hungarian composer, managed to achieve something exceptional in the music of the 20th century– uniquely to combine Western classical music with the richness of the folklore of Central Europe. In 1893-1899 he lived in Bratislava, where his mother engaged excellent music teachers for him. He was influenced by the rich musical life of the city and he was advised by his friend Ernst von Dohnányi. Both were students in the famous secondary school in the former Clare Convent on Klariská street. (See pp. 42-43).

❹ Joseph Haydn (1732-1809)

This famous composer was born in a small Austrian village just 20 km from Bratislava. For nearly 30 years he acted as conductor of the orchestra of Prince Eszterházy. Haydn gave several performances in Eszterházy Palace on Kapitulská street and it was here he introduced the local première of his opera "La Canterina". Among his most noted performances is his conducting of the court orchestra at the ball in Grassalkovich's Palace in 1772 dedicated to the favourite daughter of Maria Theresa, Maria Christine and her husband Albert of Saxe-Teschen.

❷ Franz Liszt (1811-1886)

One of the greatest of pianists, Liszt began his career in Bratislava, where he gave his first public concert in 1820 at the age of nine. He played to local aristocrats in de Pauli Palace on Ventúrska street where a memorial plaque is located (See pp. 40-41). It was these noblemen who later supported him in his studies in Vienna. Liszt had many friends in the town and frequently came on vis-

❺ Johann Nepomuk Hummel (1778-1837)

Hummel was born in Bratislava on Klobučnícka street; the house where he lived is still to be seen there. When he was seven, the family moved to Vienna. Mozart was so enthusiastic about his talent that he decided to give him classes. At the age of nine he made his first public appearance in a concert by Mozart which was a huge success. Later he became a conductor of Prince Eszterházy's court orchestra at Eisenstadt where Haydn had previously gained renown. Then he lived in Weimar and was

its. He gave in all fifteen concerts here. He was a member of St. Martin's Church Music Society and in 1884 he conducted his own Coronation Mass in the Cathedral.

a close friend of Goethe. In his time he was regarded as one of the greatest of European composers and pianists. (See pp. 60-61).

6 Ludwig van Beethoven (1770-1827)

Along with others in Bratislava, the Keglevich family befriended Beethoven. A talented pianist, Babetta Keglevich, a daughter of Count Keglevich, regularly attended Beethoven's classes in Vienna. In 1796 Beethoven dedicated several compositions to her. In the same year he gave concerts in Bratislava to several families of aristocrats, including the Keglevich family, in their palace on Panská street, today occupied by the Danish Embassy.

7 Anton Rubinstein (1829-1894)

The talented Russian pianist accepted an invitation from the Eszterházy family and at the age of 22 spent the summer of 1847 in their palace. The palace is situated on the Hlavné námestie (the Main Square), bears the name of Kutscherfeld Palace and is today occupied by the French Embassy. Rubinstein as a famous composer and pianist gave concerts in the city several times. In 1885 he and Franz Liszt performed a concert together.

8 Heinrich Marschner (1795-1861)

As a young man in 1816, this important German opera composer accepted an offer to become a music teacher and a conductor of Count Zichy's court orchestra in Bratislava. He lived in Bratislava up to 1820 during which period he composed his first famous operas. He continued his career in Dresden and later in Hannover where he became director of the opera. He had a strong influence on Wagner who later overshadowed him. Zichy Palace can still be seen on Ventúrska street.

9 Ernst von Dohnányi (1877-1960)

This important Hungarian composer was born in Bratislava in a family with a long musical tradition. They were acquainted with a number of prominent musicians

who visited them and played together. Thanks to this inspiring environment, the young composer developed a life-long love for chamber music. Later, famous composers became his music teachers until he himself became one of them. Along with Bartók, he studied at the secondary school in the former Clare Convent on Klariská street (See pp. 42-43).

10 Franz Schmidt (1874-1939)

Franz Schmidt was also a native of Bratislava. The site of the house he lived in is now occupied by the building of the Ministry of Culture on the SNP Square; his memorial plaque is displayed on its side wall. In 1888, his family moved to Vienna where he further developed his talent and built his career. He was one of the most famous Austrian composers of the 20th century and acted as Director and Chancellor of the Universität für Musik und darstellende Kunst and a teacher of a number of famous artists.

Traditions of Wine

With neighbouring Vienna (650 hectares), these are the only European capitals that today possess so many vineyards. These are beautiful places to walk and cycle.

1 Typical Cultivars

In the Small Carpathians wine-producing region, the production of white wine predominates over that of red wine. White wines find their ideal climatic conditions here. The cultivars as well as the climate are similar to those in Austria and Germany and excellent dry white wines are produced here. Traditional white cultivars are Welschriesling, Riesling, Gewürztraminer, Silvaner, Grüner Veltliner, Sauvignon blanc and Pinot gris. Blaufränkisch, St. Laurenz and Cabernet Sauvignon are among the traditional red cultivars.

🔗 mrvastanko.sk	🔗 elesko.sk
🔗 karpatskaperla.sk	🔗 vinomatysak.sk

2 Wine Glasses

Bratislava was known as a town of several ethnic groups. Natives here spoke German, Hungarian and Slovak. These groups of residents also had slightly different traditions as far as wine was concerned. The language a guest spoke determined the volume by which his favourite wine was served. German-speakers would usually drink 0.25 l (Viertel), Hungarian-speakers 0.3 l (három-three deci) and Slovak-speakers 0.2 l (dva-two deci). In Austria, Hungary and Slovakia, these units are still in use today.

3 Vineyards

Within its territory, Bratislava still encompasses extensive areas of vineyards. An area of 1000 hectares stretches over the lower slopes of the Small Carpathians.

4 Wine Route

The Small Carpathians Wine Route has its start in Rača, a former vine-growing village, which is now a part of the city. It goes through vineyards at the foot of the Small Carpathian Mountains, passes through picturesque villages and historical towns and past castles and chateaux. It passes by many well-known restaurants, wine cellars, pottery workshops, etc. The Wine Route ends at the romantic castle of Smolenice, about 60 km from Bratislava (p. 124).

🔗 mvc.sk

5 First Sparkling Wine

Bratislava was the first place outside of France where sparkling wine was produced by the méthode champenoise. In 1825, Johann Fischer founded a winery and became the first to produce it here. In 1875 the factory was purchased by the Hubert company and adopted its present name. Following success in the world's exhibitions in the 19th century, they were exported to markets all over the world. Sparkling wines from Bratislava were included on the wine list on the Titanic. High-quality sparkling wines are still produced here today.

✉ The History of Viticulture in Bratislava

The tradition of viticulture in the city is as old as the city itself. Celts and Romans produced wine in this region. The first written record of viticulture dates from the 13th century. In the 15th century the majority of residents were involved in the production of wine and in the 16th century the local wines were exported to a number of regions in Europe. There was a custom that the kings and their families took part in the grape harvest in Bratislava.

hubertsekt.sk
hacaj.sk

6 Museum of Viticulture

In the heart of the Old Town, just next to the Old Town Hall in Apponyi Palace, is located a very interesting museum which documents the rich history of viticulture in Bratislava from the past up to today. The Mediaeval cellars form an integral part of the museum.

7 Courtyards

Today, a number of houses in the Old Town still maintain their former wine cellars and courtyards in a good condition. In some of them, the old presses can even be found. Today, these former wine cellars and courtyards have been transformed into numerous restaurants, antique-shops, galleries or bars which together create the special intimate atmosphere of the Old Town. In getting to know the city, you should certainly not miss out on these romantic corners, or you will otherwise deprive yourself of many pleasant surprises.

8 The Grape Harvest

At weekends in the second half of September the region around Bratislava is busy with the grape harvest and the festivals associated with it. Nearly every village has its own grape festival but the best-known are those in the small towns of Pezinok and Modra. Folk music can be heard everywhere, and dance groups in typical folk costumes give their performances; in addition to wine, a traditional not-yet-ferment-

ed wine called "burčiak" is drunk and a local speciality – roast goose and "lokše" pancakes is on offer (see p. 81).

9 Festival of Young Wine

This ancient tradition is associated with the festival of Saint Martin, the patron saint of Bratislava.

On 11th November, Saint Martin's day, in St. Ladislas' Chapel in the Primate's Palace (see pp. 22-25), the young wine is blessed. Subsequently, the mayors of Bratislava and the surrounding wine-producing villages declare the festival which lasts for two days open. Wine producers from the region offer their young wines, various local specialities, craftsmen sell their products and all this is happens to a background of folk songs and music.

visit.bratislava.sk

10 Days of Open Wine Cellars

Every year in the mid November and mid May, the doors of sixty wine cellars in villages and small towns along the Small Carpathians Wine Route stay open for two days (Friday and Saturday). As this activity has become very popular, the number of visitors is limited and it is necessary to buy tickets in advance, along with a glass and a map. The ticket serves as admission to a sampling ad libidem of the products of the wine producers. Tickets are available in wine shops and tourist information centres.

mvc.sk

Coronation Ceremonies

1 Castle
Bratislava Castle was one of seats of the kings of

the Hungarian Kingdom. Any time that the king visited the town, he stayed in the Castle; this was true also for the coronation period. In the Castle also, the crown jewels were kept under guard. The procession formed in the Castle and descended to the town for the coronation ceremony in the decorated St. Martin's Cathedral.

2 King's Coronation Ceremony
The ceremony in St. Martin's Cathedral was the first part of the coronation and it lasted longer than two hours. The introduction, recommendation, royal oath and anointment of the future king were performed in a ceremonial atmosphere interspersed with prayers and the singing of a large choir. At the end, the royal insignia - sword, sceptre, orb and the holy crown - were presented to the king.

3 Coronation Procession
From St. Martin's Cathedral, the newly-crowned king accompanied by religious dignitaries, aristocracy, knights and trumpeters and a noisy excited crowd progressed on horseback through the streets of the Old Town and continued to the Franciscan Church.

4 Conferring Knighthoods
The first stop of the newly-crowned king was at the Franciscan Church which is the oldest in the city. Here, the king dubbed selected men of the aristocracy Knights of the Order of the Golden Spur.

5 Swearing the Oath to the People
Through St. Michael's Gate the king with his entourage processed outside the city walls. Here, in a large open space, a crowd of people gathered to hear him swear the "Oath to the People" before the Archbishop. Then, after taking the oath, he scattered gold coins into the crowd and continued along the walls towards the Danube.

6 Oath to the Land
The final part of the coronation ceremonial was the "Oath to the Land" which took place on the coronation mound close to the Danube. The mound was made up of soil brought from all parts of the Hungarian Kingdom. The king on horseback, to the pealing of bells, salvoes, fanfares and the cheers of the crowd, brandished his sword to all four sides, by which action he swore to defend the land against enemy attacks and to bring to it peace and calm.

🏛 Coronations Today

Although Slovakia is now a republic, Bratislava remains proud of its past and the coronations of kings are still very popular. The Coronation Festival always takes place in the last weekend in June. Thousands of visitors from home and abroad flock here to be part of the huge celebration and the city turns the clock back through several hundred years of history. Almost everything written in the previous pages holds true for today and so masses of folk cry "Vivat rex", drink wine from the fountains, join in the ox-roast, shout encouragement to bold knights and feast and dance in the streets.

9 Statue of Maria Theresa

In the second half of the 19th century, the coronation mound was removed and in its place on the square by the Danube a large complex of statues sculpted from white Carrara marble and devoted to Maria Theresa was built. Unfortunately, in the turbulent years after World War I, the complex was destroyed. Today there is an effort to re-build and re-install the statues. Maria Theresa was very popular in Bratislava and contributed substantially to the development of the town.

10 Saint Stephen's Crown

The Hungarian crown is associated with the name of the first Hungarian king, Stephen I, who was crowned in 1000. This event began the history of the Hungarian Kingdom, of which, up to 1918, Slovakia formed a part. The Hungarian Crown dates from the 12th century and a greatly enlarged model of it is installed on the top of the tower of St. Martin's Cathedral as a symbol of the place where coronations took place. The crown and other insignia were, with short breaks, housed in the Castle, in the period from 1552 to 1783.

7 Celebrations

Once the coronation ceremonial was over, the celebratory coronation party took place. The king, town and aristocracy dispensed sufficient money to allow everybody, including the people, to enjoy it. Fountains spraying wine were built, oxen roasted, knights' tournaments organised, theatrical performances given, as well as mock battles between ships and all around in the streets people were dancing and singing.

8 Crowns on Pavements

Several years ago, small brass crowns at several metre-intervals were fixed in the pavements in the Old Town to commemorate the coronation procession and allow everybody even today to follow in the footsteps of kings. They lead from St. Martin's Cathedral to the Franciscan Church and out beyond St. Michael's Gate.

69

MARTIN 🎨 SLOBODA

Bratislava for Children

1 Art and crafts

Bibiana – the International House for Children - is a unique institution which directs its activities towards fostering artistic creativity in children of all ages. It is housed in a palace on Panská street. It

provides access to art in a non-conventional and non-traditional manner, by way of experimental art-forms. Since artists are actively involved in

the activities organised by Bibiana, a high professional level is maintained. 🔍 2 CP 28

🔗 bibiana.sk

UĽUV – The Centre for Folk Handicrafts has its "Crafts Courtyard" on Obchodná street. It consists of five creative workshops – woodcarvers, weavers, basket-work, potters and tinkers, where children as well as adults can take part in various courses and learn how to make original Slovak folk products in the original traditional manner. 🔍 2 DA 13

🔗 uluv.sk

2 Children's playgrounds

The most beautiful playgrounds for children in the city centre can be found in the attractive surroundings of natural or historical parks. The very popular forester's house in Hill Park (p. 48, 🔍 1 AM 11) possesses, in addition to climbing frames, domestic animals and a fireplace for barbecuing. A very well-equipped playground with

a kiosk is located near the Leberfinger restaurant in Janko Kráľ Park (🔍 1 AV 23). The playground in the Medical Garden has the biggest sandpit and climbing frames. (See pp. 48-49). Incontestably the best place for children is at Partisan Meadow, alongside the trail leading to Železná studnička "the Iron Well" (See p. 73).

3 "Prešporáčik"

If you want to show children some history without them getting bored, arrange for them to have a ride in an attractive imitation of a historic car called Prešporáčik. It will drive you through the narrow streets of the Old Town and provide a commentary in many languages. It has its terminus on the Main Square where it awaits its guests every day from the end of March to the end of October.

🔗 presporacik.sk

4 Bratislava's forests

Getting out into the open air in Bratislava is not difficult, nor do you have to go far, a fact that is welcomed and made use of by local residents as well as visitors. The

Kamzík Hill (440m), (p. 123) is only 10 minutes from the city centre. There is a summer bobsleigh run, very popular with children, and right alongside it a ski slope. The nearby riding service provides horse-rides for children. The top of the hill is occupied by one of Bratislava's dominant features – the TV Tower. (See pp. 54-55). It has one attraction that does not escape the curiosity of children; the tower holds a rotating restaurant which provides a spectacular view over the whole city.

5 Bratislava ZOO & Dinopark

Bratislava's Zoo is located in Mlynská dolina valley, close to the motorway in the western part of the city. At present, more than a thousand animals representing nearly 150 animal species are to be found here. Part of the Zoo is a unique DinoPark; in three hectares of woodland, 27 life-size models of various dinosaurs, which can move and produce sounds, are installed. Amongst other attractions there is a paleontological playground in which children can themselves discover and dig out a skeleton of dinosaur from the sand. ⊠ 1 AB 15

🔗 zoobratislava.sk

6 Festival of Water Sprites

Every year, on a Saturday in early June, a long procession of people in green fancy dress and masks winds through the city. It is an International Festival of Water Sprites which brings together sprites of all sizes and ages. The procession starts at the river bank and goes all over the old town before finishing on the promenade where various competitions are held. The tastiest contest involves making a soup from fish from the Danube, an event which is most not missed by teams from neighbouring countries.

🔗 visit.bratislava.sk

7 Children's museum (Detské múzeum)

The Children's Museum is located in the premises of the Slovak National Museum on Vajanského nábrežie in Bratislava. In addition to exhibition premises and very interesting and educational exhibitions, the museum also contains a children's laboratory, workshops, a play room for children, children's theater and a patisserie. The Children's Museum is open daily from 10 a.m. to 6 p.m. It is an excellent way of supplementing your children's education in a playful and interactive way. Have fun and use your free time well. Vajanského nábrežie 2, ⊠ 2 DC 30

🔗 detskemuzeum.sk

8 Children's Theatre and Puppet Theatre

Children very much enjoy theatre and the famous Aréna Theatre in Janko Kráľ Park has several plays for children in its repertoire. The performances are held in the mornings. ⊠ 1 AZ 32

🔗 divadloarena.sk.

Bratislava Puppet Theatre on Dunajská Street is a well-established theatre with a long tradition and a number of awards. Thanks to its major creative potential, the theatre is always busy. In addition to performances, children can visit the workshops where puppets are made. ⊠ 2 DH 19

🔗 babkovedivadlo.sk

9 Ballet

Bratislava is a city with a rich musical tradition and the same holds true for opera and ballet. Both are provided at a very high quality and people are accustomed to attending frequently. Even classes of schoolchildren go to the ballet and opera. Performances for children are given in the mornings (See p. 32).

🔗 snd.sk

10 Salaš

About 25 km north of Bratislava, the Príroda (Nature) organic farm in the style of an original shepherd's cottage (salaš) is to be found in the woods outside the little town of Stupava. Although you are only a stone's throw away from the town, the sound of sheep bells and the sight of the original wooden cottage beguile you into thinking otherwise. A special sheep's cheese called bryndza and other sorts of cheeses are produced here by traditional methods and there are typical dishes on the menu served in these authentic surroundings.

🔗 biofarma.sk

Sports and Leisure

1 Hills & Forests

Bratislava is one of the few cities where the forests start right in the city. The Kamzík Hill (440m), (See p. 123) accessible by car or the 203 trolleybus from the Crowne Plaza Hotel, is the starting point for pleasant bike trips and

hiking and also an excellent site for a picnic with friends. There is a popular summer bob-sleigh run and in winter a ski slope which also offers an opportunity for sledging. Just next to the bob-sleigh run is a ropes course among mature tall trees, ideally suited to active recreation and adventure. Here, you can push yourself to your limits.

🍃 lanoland.sk

🍃 cyklotrasy.sk

2 Rafting

One of the sports that Slovaks never leave the Olympic Games without medals is white-water

southern part of Bratislava. The two parallel watercourses with their regulated volume of water, waterfalls and boulders are frequently used by the public for rafting. All the necessary equipment is available for hire in the area.

🍃 raftovanie.sk

3 Relaxx

A new centre for keeping you in a healthy condition can be found opposite the Aupark shopping centre. At Fitfactory you can expend your energy and then have it restored. A swimming pool, the biggest fitness centre in the whole of Slovakia, saunas and whirlpools, an indoor golf course and many other attractions are to be found under one roof. Your children will be well looked after in the indoor children's playground and you can regain whatever you have lost in an organic restaurant.
📷 1 AZ 36

🍃 relaxx.sk

4 National Tennis Centre

Although Slovakia is a small country, it possesses a large number of excellent tennis players and tennis is one of the most popular sports. Tennis courts are to be found scattered all over the city. The newly-built National Tennis Centre offers not only top-quality conditions for tennis tournaments, such as the Davis Cup, but also for other sports and cultural events and its facilities are open to the public. Part of the NTC is a well-known tennis school. 📷 1 BK 8

🍃 ntc.sk

slalom. This is in part due to the artificial water canals with white- water. One of highest quality white-water centres in Europe, where world championships take place, was constructed on the Danube near the village of Čunovo in the

5 Bicycles and In-Line Skates

That Bratislavans are sport-loving and active people is obvious to anybody visiting the Danube embankment on a summer afternoon (See p. 121). A particularly popular section of the embankment begins by the Old Bridge where thousands of activity-loving people on their bikes or roller-blades can be found. The embankment runs along the river and leads you out of the city and how far you go is up to you. Usually people get to the city limits – an artificial white water canal in Čunovo 17 km from the city and then they turn round.

🔗 cyklotrasy.sk

6 A Green Valley

Železná studnička (the Iron Well) is a beauti-

ful valley on the Western side of the Kamzík Hill (See p. 123). It is famous for several ponds which freeze over in winter and became a paradise for amateur figure-skaters and hockey-players. All along the valley are wooden shelters and open air fireplaces ideal for a family picnic. The surrounding meadows and woodland attract bikers in summer and cross-country skiing enthusiasts in winter. The valley is connected with the top of

the Kamzík Hill by a chair-lift that accommodates also bicycles.

7 Slovakia Ring

Automobile racing enthusiasts will come into their own at the Slovakia Ring circuit, which is one of the longest in Europe. Just 30km from Bratislava you can rent a sports car and get a taste of what it's like behind the wheel, or just be a passenger in the Race Taxi.

🔗 slovakiaring.sk

8 Bowling

Devotees of this relaxing sport will find the very well-equipped Brunswick Bowling Club on the second floor of the shopping and entertainment centre Aupark. 📍 1 AT 35

🔗 aupark.sk

9 Golf

The Bratislava Golf & Country Club in the village of Bernolákovo just 16 km from the city offers the closest opportunity for golfing relaxation. The 18-hole golf course lies in the historic park of the Baroque chateau set in the beautiful countryside.

🔗 golf.sk

10 Ice Hockey

Ice hockey is probably the most popular sport in Slovakia; its popularity is perhaps partly due to international success. However, ice hockey is not just a spectator sport. A number of people play it with their friends on frozen lakes in winters and in stadiums all the year round. There are three roofed stadiums in Bratislava providing fa-

cilities to the public, of which the Ondrej Nepela Stadium on Odbojárov street is the biggest. It is the home-stadium for one of the most successful ice-hockey clubs in Slovakia - Slovan Bratislava. 📍 1 BL 11

🔗 hcslovan.sk

Going Out

Cafés

1 Roland Caffé

One of the best-known coffeehouses in Bratislava is to be found on the ground floor of a bank, in the Art Nouveau style. The high ceilings of the former banking hall and the large windows overlooking the Main Square make it eminently suited for simply sitting and watching the world go by and enjoying whatever's in front of you. They serve cakes and desserts of their own making. Behind the bar, they've kept a large safe from the original bank.
Hlavné nám. 5, 2 CT 24

🔗 rolandcaffe.sk

2 Kaffee Mayer

Herr Mayer, a supplier to the royal court in Vienna, opened this café in 1873. Since then, the atmosphere inside the coffeehouse hasn't changed all that much. In the past, just as now, it was one of the city's icons and for many people Sunday afternoon wouldn't be Sunday afternoon without a visit to Kaffee Mayer. The moment you step inside you realise they really know about cakes here. There's a wide variety of fresh cakes made in the basement confectionery and supplied to the café. This is a Kaffee with a capital K.
Hlavné nám. 4, 2 CT 24

🔗 kaffemayer.sk

3 Schokocafé Maximilian

It is the name of this coffeehouse overlooking the main square, with a gallery in the mezzanine, that gives it away. Besides coffee, many different varieties of hot chocolate drinks are served here; chocolate even flows from a little fountain. However, chocolate can also be had in a solid form; a large selection of pralines from famous producers is available here. Good news for clean-air lovers– this is a smoke-free zone. Hlavné nám. 6, 2 CT 24

4 Café Café

A modern style coffeehouse at the intersection of two important streets in the Old Town. Especially in summer, due to its pleasant terrace

decorated with palms and provided with comfortable chairs, the café attracts the young and smart, wanting to see and be seen. The delicious coffee and even more tasty cakes then also tempt others. Ventúrska 1, 2 CR 26

🔗 cafecafe.sk

5 Café Grande

Soak up the pleasant atmosphere of a modern café that offers a wide selection of coffees and freshly made cakes, in an elegant classic interior decorated in warm pastel tones. While strolling around the Old Town, recharge your batteries and stimulate your taste buds with an invigorating coffee and poppy seed and black cherry strudel, Sacher chocolate cake, punch or cream cake. Alternatively, have a refreshing cold beer, glass of wine, soft drink or cocktail. Our terrace is a relaxing and comfortable oasis right on the Main Square.
Hlavné námestie 3, 2 CT 24

🔗 cafegrande.sk

6 Café L´aura

Experience an interesting aura at the stylish L´aura café in Bratislava. The cosiness of this café is in its antique furnishings, stone floor, wooden chairs, comfortable armchairs and decorative artefacts. The complementary background music, interesting interior and the rich choice of drinks on offer are an inspiration in the hustle and bustle of city life. When the weather is warmer, you can sit outside and take in the atmosphere of the monumental St. Martin's Cathedral, which is particularly charming when illuminated at night.
Rudnayovo námestie 4, 2 CP 27

7 Lancia

A trendy café where the feel and flavours change throughout the day. In the morning you will be welcomed by a hearty breakfast, while later on it

becomes the perfect place for combining a business meeting with a rich culinary lunch or dinner. The café oozes with the spirit of the Lancia car make, and offers a fantastic range of light meals, drinks and excellent coffees, guaranteed to satisfy even the more demanding patrons. The terrace is just a skip way from the main tourist drag. Ventúrska 1, 🔲 2 CQ 26

lanciacafe.sk

8 Café Antik

A tiny coffeehouse on the main artery of the Old Town Corso, elegant and tastefully fitted out with various pieces of antique furniture. It looks like it's been here for at least 120 years. It is popular with intellectuals and artists; it has a life of its own with a clientele of regulars. Its atmosphere, style and chatty waiters are reminiscent of old caffés in Italy.
Rybárska brána 2, 🔲 2 CU 24

9 Chocolaterie pod Michalom

Chocolate -the genuine article - is served here, not just cocoa. And it is prepared in dozens of different ways - even with the addition of aphrodisiacs. Anyone who hasn't seen the film Chocolat won't understand. You come here to commit a sin - and go away addicted to chocolate. There is probably no place in the city with a greater proportion of devotees. Anyone not satisfied just with chocolate in a liquid state can enjoy delicious pralines. Tiny, always crowded, and non-smoking.
Michalská 6, 🔲 2 CR 21

10 Café Shtoor

Anyone looking for a trendy Slovak cafe with a touch of national history should make their way to Café Shtoor. The cafe is particularly popular with the students of nearby faculties, who sit under the watchful images of the hero of the national renaissance, Ľudovít Štúr, chatting about difficult exams at school, or just having fun and a gossip.
Štúrova ulica 8, 🔲 2 DC 25

www.shtoor.sk

🍰 Cakes and Desserts

1 Strudel

This is made from filo pastry that needs to be really thin - almost transparent. There are three kinds available – apple with walnuts, poppy seed with wild cherries or grapes depending on the season, and curd with raisins.

2 "Krémeš"

Cream cakes are made of two layers of puff pastry filled with vanilla cream and whipped cream. They can be sprinkled with icing sugar or covered with chocolate.

3 Chestnut Purée

This is a popular munch made from boiled, peeled chestnuts. After the addition of sugar and rum the chestnuts are extruded and served with whipped cream.

4 "Palacinky"

These are similar to French crêpes, only thicker. Usually filled with jam, walnut or curd cheese and decorated with chocolate and whipped cream.

5 Pressburger Beugel

This is Bratislava's best-known cake. The famous bent Pressburg rolls called beugel are made of butter pastry with walnut or poppy seed filling.

6 Walnut Cake

Butter pastry, covered with a layer of walnut filling with rum and raisins, is shaped into a roll, brushed with egg and baked. This long roll is then cut into smaller pieces like strudel.

7 "Veterník"

This bun-sized cake is made from puff pastry. The cavity in the round hollow cake is filled with vanilla cream. The cake is glazed with caramel topping.

8 "Doboška"

Several layers of pastry are filled with chocolate cream and topped with a chocolate glaze.

9 "Šúlance"

Small rolls of potato pastry are first boiled and then served sprinkled with ground walnuts, poppy seeds or curd cheese, sugar and butter.

10 "Gulky"

Balls of potato pastry filled with fruit in season (apricots, plums) are boiled and sprinkled with a mixture of butter-fried bread crumbs or curd cheese with sugar and butter.

Typical Restaurants

1 Zylinder €€€

The new star among quality restaurants not far from the Opera provides a unique combination of the very best of cuisine from the era of the Austro-Hungarian monarchy, which Bratislava was the centre of, and modern culinary art. Everything on the menu is so good, it's hard to make a choice. Just try everything, complemented by some fine Slovak wine.
Hviezdoslavovo nám. 19,
📍 2 CU 26

    zylinder.sk

2 Leberfinger €€

An inn dating from the 17th century is situated across from the Old Town on the right bank of the Danube. It was here where merchants stopped before crossing the river and entering the town. Leberfinger focuses on the traditional Pressburg cuisine - a symbiosis of the best of Slovakia, Austria and Hungary. In summer there is a pleasant terrace shaded by an old spreading tree and at the back of the building a playground popular with children.
Viedenská cesta 257, 📍 1 AT 31

    leberfinger.sk

3 Modrá hviezda €€

On the steep narrow little street leading up to the Castle, in an 18th century house just a few metres from the house where the famous Hungarian poet Petöfi lived. Partly in cellars hewn out of the castle rock. A cosy restaurant with a special atmosphere offering the best dishes from the Pressburg cuisine. It is an ideal place to stop for lunch on your way up to the Castle or, on your return from the Castle, to dine in the romantic candlelight.
Beblavého 14, 📍 2 CM 27

    modrahviezda.sk

4 Prešburg €€

The ´culinaria domestica´ on offer at this restaurant includes various Slovak specialities like 'Bryndzové halušky' ('Bryndza' gnocchi), 'parenica' steamed cheese, bean soup, chicken broth, Tartar steak, goulash, 'Pörkölt' (meat stew), 'Strapačky'

(sauerkraut and gnocchi), roast chicken, goose or pork. You can quench your thirst with any of the many beers and wines on offer. The authentic photographs and paintings of old Bratislava, and newspaper excerpts from various periods of the city's past adorn the interior. In the summer you can enjoy sitting on the terrace.
Michalská 4, 📍 2 CR 22

    presburgrestaurant.sk

5 Pivovar Záhrada €€

One of the largest establishments in the city, capable of catering with ease for 400 thirsty patrons. That's because here the beer is brewed directly on site. The fresh beer together with regional specialities is a tried and tested recipe for filling up the bar with locals. Even with such a large capacity, best to book a table in advance. In the summer, everything tastes even better under the shade of the large trees in the beer garden. Dunajská 21, 📍 2 DI 19

    mestianskypivovar.sk

6 Bakchus Vináreň €€€

A discreet little house, but concealing a 100m long brick-walled cellar, which was built under the vineyards back in the 17th century. It draws people from all around thanks to the local cuisine and the fine wines on offer from the Little Carpathians. The menu is a celebration of the very best that this region has to offer.
Hloboká cesta 5,
🔲 1 AR 15

⤏ bakchus-vinaren.sk

7 Gazdovský dvor €€

Located in the small Perugia Hotel in a side-street in the Old Town. A cosy restaurant fitted out in a farm-style offers the best of the Hungarian cuisine popular with and in no way foreign to Slovaks. A newly-built part, styled like a shepherd's hut, tempts you to spend a lively evening with live gypsy music.
Zelená 5, 🔲 2 CR 25

⤏ perugia.sk

8 Bratislavský meštiansky pivovar €€

Where good beer is brewed, the cuisine they 'brew up' must also be good. This small local brewery follows on in the tradition of the well-known city brewery called "Die Bürgerliche Brauerei", producing beer with state-of-the-art technology accompanied by a selection of meals prepared using traditional Presburg (Bratislava) recipes. Creamy beef sirloin, dill sauce with dump-

lings, pork knuckle, goose and many more local delicacies accompanied by the fresh aroma of hops all around, is the kind of gastronomic experience you can expect at this three-floor establishment. Drevená 8, 🔲 2 CT 16

⤏ mestianskypivovar.sk

9 Sladovňa €€

A bastion of beer. Definitely worth a visit if you enjoy a good beer and some home-style cooking, home-grown pork specialities, or tasty titbits with a beer or glass of wine. You can relish over your favourite beer on solid oak seating and tables, and even have your own mini-keg brought to your table so you can tap it yourself. With its selection of Zlatý Bažant, Krušovice, Heineken, Paulaner and Guinness, the spacious Sladovna 'beer bar' can easily deal with large groups of tourists.
Ventúrska 5, 🔲 2 CQ 25

⤏ sladovna.com

10 Beer Palace €€

In this truly historical beer palace just a skip away from the Opera, you can expect exactly what is promised – excellent, fresh, non-pasteurised beer from copper tanks, tasty traditional regional cuisine and concerts in the evenings with various live acts. After a roast duck, some 'Halušky' gnocchi, or a game goulash, only empty plates remain.
Gorkého 5, 🔲 2 CX 25

⤏ beerpalace.sk

ℹ️ Prices for a three-course meal without drinks:	
€	EUR 10
€€	EUR 15
€€€	EUR 20

Traditional Dishes

1 "Bryndzové halušky"

The much-vaunted Slovak national dish has its origin in the mountainous regions and divides natives and visitors alike into those who love it and those who "choose not to". Noodles are made from grated raw potato, flour and salt; they are like little gnocchi and are served with a fresh soft sheep's cheese called bryndza which is an original product of Slovakia and not found anywhere else in the world, sour cream and fried bacon. The gnocchi are made in a number of variations and those served with fermented cabbage and bacon are known as strapačky.

2 Wiener Schnitzel

Although it has Vienna in its name, it is just as popular in Bratislava as in Vienna 60 km to the southwest of Bratislava. The original fillet is from veal; however, it can just as well be made from pork. On Sunday mornings a lot of Bratislavans are woken by the sound of "beaten fillets" coming from their neighbours.

The meat processed in this way is thinner and tenderer; it is covered in flour, then dipped in beaten egg and finally in breadcrumbs and fried. Wiener schnitzel is usually served with coleslaw.

3 Chicken Soup

Slovakia is a land where life without soup is unthinkable. Chicken soup is an institution in which generations of Slovaks have been brought up and there's no sign this is going to change anytime soon. Just wander past a few open windows and you will surely smell it. Its genuine strong taste and golden colour comes from meat and a variety of root vegetables and thin home-made noodles.

4 "Kapustnica"

This is a typical winter dish which combines just about all the best ingredients you can put together in winter. The soup is served, in particular, on New Year's Day but some also have it on Christmas Eve. Its main ingredients are fresh fermented cabbage and dried funghi; sometimes sausage, dried plums and other delicacies are added to it. It is a thick soup served with a spoonful of sour cream and a slice of bread.

5 Goulash

Once you become familiar with the history of the region and look at the map it comes as no surprise that Hungarian cuisine is so popular in this here. Everybody has his or her own recipe for cooking goulash; however its basic ingredients are always the same – an onion, garlic, pork and beef and spices, especially shiny-red paprika. It is served with bread dumplings.

6 "Bryndzové pirohy"

This scarf-like pasta, like gnocchi, filled with a special sheep's cheese called bryndza, comes from the mountainous areas of Slovakia. It's made from a mixture of boiled potatoes and flour and looks like big ravioli. Often they are filled with fresh sheep's cheese with potatoes and are served with a cream sauce with dill and fried onion or bacon.

7 Grilled Trout

Traditional fish dishes in Slovakia consist of freshwater fish from the surrounding rivers and lakes. Trout is the most common fish on the menu; it is usually grilled with garlic, butter and various herbs.

8 Fried Cheese

This is a very common and popular cheap dish available in almost every restaurant.

A slice of Edam or Camembert is covered in breadcrumbs and fried in oil. Slovaks like it with pommes frites or boiled potatoes and tartare sauce.

9 Chicken "Paprikáš"

This chicken stew is another dish originating from Hungarian cuisine. It is cooked from chicken, onion, garlic, white wine, sour cream - and paprika, of course. Gnocchi which differ from the Slovak ones in that they are made from only flour and water are usually served as a side dish.

10 Roast Goose, Goose Liver and "Lokše"

When the season starts, the whole of Bratislava pours out to the surrounding villages na hus - to have a goose. There's an art to roasting a goose properly and not everyone can do it. The best chefs guard their recipes very carefully.

A soft goose liver is served as a starter. Roast goose is served with lokše pancakes and often with stewed red cabbage. Lokše pancakes are a local speciality similar to pancakes but are made from potatoes and roasted without oil.

🍷 Typical Drinks

1 Vinea
A refreshing soft drink from natural grape-must, first produced in 1974. Currently, the drink is experiencing a comeback. It is natural, healthy and Slovak.

2 Karpatské Brandy Special
This exclusive liquor gets matured in small oak casks for at least five years and then for an additional three. The XO mark is matured for a total of fifteen years and its quality is comparable with the world's best.

3 Borovička
Traditional Slovak spirit from the mountainous regions made from Juniper berries resembles gin. The best-known brand is Spišská Borovička.

4 Slivovica
A typical product distilled from plums from the central and southern regions of Slovakia. It usually contains 53 % alcohol. Bošácka Slivovica is of the highest quality.

5 Demänovka
A natural Slovak herbal liqueur made from fourteen different herbs and sweetened with honey. It is enjoyed as aperitif or digestif.

6 Kofola
This non-alcoholic beverage similar to coca-cola with its origin in the communist era is experiencing a revival. It is produced exclusively from natural ingredients and served on draught, like beer.

7 "Burčiak"
In Autumn this drink is available everywhere. It is in the transitional stage between a grape-must and a wine. It has reached the stage of fermentation and already contains alcohol. Don't drink it like juice.

8 Mulled Wine
The Christmas Market would be unimaginable without this traditional winter drink. Spices enhance its pleasant flavour.

9 Beer
Beer is drunk well and often. Draught Slovak or Czech beers are available almost everywhere. Beers from anywhere else don't get much of a look in here. Most beers are lagers or dark beers.

10 Wine
Even today, there are still vineyards to be found within the city. The climate is most suited to dry white wines. In recent years, the quality of the wines has increased markedly.

Top Restaurants

1 Carnevalle €

You can find the very best cuts of beef, veal, pork and lamb in Bratislava right here. An excellent location in the Old Town, a well balanced mix of regional and international cuisine, excellent recipes and a high standard of quality, combine to ensure a true culinary experience. If you don't get enough at the restaurant, you can also buy some quality meat to take home. Hivezdoslavovo nám 20, 🔲 2 CT 27

⮑ carnevalle.sk

2 Zylinder €

The new star among quality restaurants not far from the Opera provides a unique combination of the very best of cuisine from the era of the Austro-Hungarian monarchy, which Bratislava was the centre of, and modern culinary art. Everything on the menu is so good, it's hard to make a choice. Just try everything, complemented by some fine Slovak wine..
Hviezdoslavovo nám. 19, 🔲 2 CU 26

⮑ zylinder.sk

3 Fou Zoo €€

As soon as the door opens, it becomes immediately clear that this is a special place. The young Slovak chef who has gained his experience in some of the best restaurants in London, shows that gastronomy truly is an art. A perfect fusion of Asian and European cuisine. It's almost a pity to eat what is presented to you on the plate. Once you do taste it, though, Fou Zoo will have you in its grasp and won't let you go. After that, it is just Fou Zoo and the rest.

Ševčenkova 34, 🔲 3 FG 12

⮑ fouzoo.sk

4 Albrecht €€€

This restaurant is part of a hotel, but it is also popular with many customers from outside the hotel. There was an absence of top quality cuisine in this district. In a short space of time the Albrecht had gained in popularity as a business restaurant. The menu is divided into day menu and an evening menu, which is a novelty in Slovakia. Even the Sunday brunch has already become popular. Apart from fantastic international cuisine, a pleasant restaurant environment, a garden, a terrace and very accomodating staff, it also has very good parking.
Mudroňova 82, 🔲 2 CC 25

⮑ hotelalbrecht.com

5 Le Monde €€€

This highly ambitious restaurant represents the absolute peak in Bratislava. Even its location can hardly be rivalled– a noble historical house right by the Opera House. The trendy, delicately elegant interior matches well with the creations on plates where the modern combines with traditional cuisines from various parts of Europe and Asia. The visitor goes to Le Monde to experience a culinary adventure – one which is best enjoyed from the first floor balcony overlooking the square and the Opera House.
Hviezdoslavovo nám 26, 🔲 2 CU 26

⮑ lemonde.sk

6 Matyšák Restaurant €€

This modern hotel built over historical wine cellars was commissioned by a well-known family of wine producers. The non-smoking wine restaurant under the original brick arches reverts to the old Bratislava tradition of regional cuisine using wine and seasonal variations. The rustic style combines well with the live folk music in the evenings. Right alongside it is a huge wine

store (45,000 bottles) in historical cellars - ideal for sampling the Matyšák wine products.
Pražská 15, 🔲 1 AS 14

7 Messina €€

This - probably the most beautiful of all the restaurants in Bratislava - is housed in the lovely boutique hotel in the neighbourhood of the Old Town. The elegant classical furniture, the dark colours and warm light create a very cosy atmosphere. Due to its location – despite being close to the main tourist routes –this is an ideal place for undisturbed conversation and business meetings. Taking its name from a famous Italian painter is a sign that this is a restaurant ruled by a creative Italian cuisine.
Tobrucká 4, 🔲 2 DC 28

8 Flowers €€€

A sunny restaurant in the romantic courtyard of Erdödy Palace. A sense of airiness and freedom and the presence of a little bit of nature will greet you, not just on the plate but also in the interior. The restaurant is decorated with pictures from the well-known Flowers series by Andy Warhol and the glass ceiling evokes a feeling of unlimited space. The Mediterranean cuisine will undoubtedly attract you with the excellent taste of its salads, home-made pasta and fresh home-baked breads. Let yourself be spoiled by the best restaurant of 2007.
Ventúrska 1 , 🔲 2 CQ 27

9 UFO €€€

"Floating" on the pillar of the New Bridge (Nový most), this restaurant offers a pretty unconventional experience, from where you can enjoy

a unique panoramic view of Bratislava and its surroundings from above. The restaurant interior is elegantly furnished and the menu contains a wide variety of different international dishes. The restaurant has a total of 140 seats and reservations are possible. Offering an impressive view, this restaurant is a landmark of Bratislava and represents Slovakia in the World Federation of Great Towers. Novy Most, 🔲 2 CO 36

10 Benihana €

Benihana is proof that excellent food and super entertainment go hand in hand. The food is prepared in the style of Teppanyaki right before your eyes, like some circus performance. After a display of flying prawns and knives, your mouth-watering food will land right on the plate in front of you. Come along with the kids and you'll be amazed at their appetite. Prawns will fly straight into their mouth.
Hlboká cesta 7, 🔲 1 AR 15

ℹ️ Prices for a three-course menu without drinks:	
€	EUR 30
€€	EUR 35
€€€	EUR 40
€€€€	EUR 45

Students' Haunts

🔢 Potrefená husa

This themed beer bar, right next to the University, offers a wide variety of beers and typical dishes that go well with beer. It is a popular place for students to spend their lunch break or time after classes and it is especially suited for those with deep pockets. It's a favourite spot for law students to celebrate after exams.
Šafárikovo nám 7, 🔲 2 DF 28

🔢 Café Verne

A popular stylish bar fitted out with antique furniture on the ground floor of the University of Fine Arts. However, it's not just talented artists

who meet here. In summer, it extends to a pleasant terrace under big trees which gives this part of the square the right atmosphere. This is one of the few places where simple home-made fare is on offer.
Hviezdoslavovo nám. 18, 🔲 2 CS 27

🔢 Prašná bašta

The restaurant in a circular layout in a former bastion of the town fortification is accessed through the courtyard of a historical house. A very good balance is struck between price and quality of the largely regional cuisine. Excellent evenings with live music in a style taken from between the wars. Very popular in summer due to its romantic garden in the former city moat.
Zámočnícka 11, 🔲 2 CS 20

☞ prasnabasta.sk

🔢 Next Apache

In an quiet old street just next to a small church you will discover a little corner of an old world which is popular with students and intellectuals. Here, there is a purpose and a philosophy behind everything; there are old-fashioned sofas and shelves filled with books which act as an second-hand bookshop. The coffee is Fair Trade and oc-

casionally the venue for genre music and theme evenings. You can find the events programme at www. Panenská 28, 🔲 2 CN 14

☞ nextapache.sk

🔢 1. Slovak Pub

This typical old Slovak pub is a real maze where you can learn a great deal about the history of the Slovak nation. It has an old-fashioned atmosphere, a large selection of home-made fare, the largest selection of Slovak beers in the city - and surprisingly agreeable prices. It is not only one of the largest pubs (capacity in excess of 500 people) it is also one of the best in the city. A progressive feature is that students and non-smokers are charged at reduced rates.
Obchodná 62, 🔲 2 CY 14

☞ slovakpub.sk

🔢 Café Kút

It takes an insider to find this bar, hidden in the courtyard of an old house near a former bastion of the town fortification. The tiny, cosy rooms, antique furniture, twilight and creaking wooden floor create a homely atmosphere that is difficult to resist. Live reggae concerts are held here.
Zámočnícka 11, 🔲 2 CS 20

☞ kut.prasnabasta.sk

🔢 Umelka

Umelka is a concept and there is not a single student who would fail to be familiar with it. Simply because it is located right opposite the main building of Comenius University. Typical simple meals that go best with beer are served here. And, like all proper pubs, they also serve draught kofola (see p. 81). In the one of the largest of the city's gardens, under old chestnut trees, live music is performed from Wednesday to Sunday in the country, oldies and latino rhythms, for dancing and beer-drinking. Dostojevského rad 2, 🔲 2 DG 29

🔗 umelka.sk

8 Coffee & Co

This cafe with a homely atmosphere on one of the busiest streets in the pedestrian zone is a popular place for friends to meet, where students, artists, intellectuals and also pseudo-intellectuals can just chill out over a coffee and a cake or a fresh bagel. This coffee bar also hosts various special events and expositions of contemporary artists. Laurinská 5, 🔲 2 CX 24

🔗 coffee-co.sk

9 Kafe Scherz

In the tranquil Palisády area of Bratislava you can find Art klub, where every Monday there is an artistic programme with club-like service. The pleasant colour tones, antique furnishing, paintings and timeless photographs combine to produce the atmosphere of a café for students or special-interest groups. It is often the venue for book and CD christenings, concerts, recitals, or exhibitions of established and up-and-coming artists. In the summer you can sit outside at the front or on the terrace at the back. Partizánska 2, 🔲 2 CF 24

🔗 scherz.sk

10 Bratislavská reštaurácia

You can choose from a wide range of meals and drinks in the impressive premises of the Bratislava Restaurant, also known as the Bratislava Flagship Restaurant. On entering you are welcomed by a charming 'alleyway' in the spirit of old Bratislava housing with little shops offering various products like cheese, wine and vegetables. You enter the main building in the restaurant section on the upper floor, which offers classic meals and a special lunch menu in interesting premises with a student-like atmosphere. Námestie SNP č.8, 🔲 2 CX 18

🔗 bratislavskarestauracia.sk

🍺 Pubs

1 Dubliner

A roomy Irish pub with a country atmosphere and a large fireplace, popular with foreigners living in Bratislava. Crowded during sports matches. Sedlárska 6, 🔲 2 CS 23

2 Budweiser Budvar

This huge beer parlour in the former fire brigade station is the only one to offer Budvar beer from the tank. Why not try some excellent domestic cuisine or enjoy the country music night every Cintorínska 19, 🔲 2 DL 15

3 Prazdroj

A large beer-house in a Czech style straight across from the Slovak Philharmonic. Musicans too, come here to enjoy a high-quality Czech beer and tasty Czech cuisine. Mostová 8, 🔲 2 CV 29

4 Beer Palace

Expect exactly what is promised – excellent, fresh, non-pasteurised beer from copper tanks, tasty traditional regional cuisine and concerts in the evenings with various live acts. After a roast duck, some 'Halušky' gnocchi, or a game goulash, only empty plates remain. Gorkého 5, 🔲 2 CX 25

5 Pivovar Záhrada

The fresh beer together with regional specialities is a tried and tested recipe for filling up the bar with locals. Even with such a large capacity, best to book a table in advance. In the summer, everything tastes even better under the shade of the large trees in the beer garden. Dunajská 21, 🔲 2 DI 19

6 Bratislavský meštiansky pivovar

A small brewery serving also its own special beers – Bratislava lager and 20% ABV black beer Sessler. It brews them in 500-litre casks and 'brews up' some excellent food to accompany them. Drevená 8, 🔲 2 CT 16

7 Bratislavská reštaurácia

Large interesting premises, student-like atmosphere, with a rich selection of meals and beers, such as Zlatý bažant, Heineken, Krušovice, Edelweiss, Dobré pivko, Kelt, Starobrno, Corgoň and others. Námestie SNP č.8, 🔲 2 CV 18

8 Sladovňa

Oak benches, the aroma of home-style specialities and a large selection of bottled and draft beers, as well as beer in mini kegs, which you can tap yourself. A true bastion of beer all under one roof. Ventúrska 5, 🔲 2 CQ 25

9 Kolkovňa

Traditional Czech restaurant with modern concept and Pilsner Urquell and Šariš beers. Relaxing atmosphere with outside seating in the summer overlooking the River Danube. Pribinova 8, 🔲 2 DJ 29

10 1. Slovak Pub

Zlatý bažant, Kelt, Krušovice, Dobré pivko, beer cocktails and Slovak specialities are just some of the delights offered by this large spacious pub. A place where you can enjoy a good drink of beer and also discover something about Slovakia. Obchodná 62, 🔲 2 CZ 14

Bars and Live Music

1 Sky bar

By its locality and appearance, this establishment is way above the competition. On the large terraces of the open roof in one of the tallest buildings in the Old Town, there is nothing better than to sit on a sofa surrounded by people having fun while sipping at a mojito and taking in the breathtaking view of the illuminated castle and the Old Town down below you. Hviezdoslavovo nám. 7, 🖼 2 CS 28

🔗 skybar.sk

2 Barrock

The ministry of entertainment warns you that some excellent unhealthy food and loud music is served at this rock bar. Here you can drink till you drop and feed the wild animals. Anyone looking for a real rocking night out with live music, excellent DJs and spicy food, should definitely pop into Barrock. Sedlárska 1, 🖼 2 CR 23

🔗 barrock.sk

3 Rio Grande Restaurant

The feel of this bar complex is unique. Sample

a classic Caipirinha Rio, or any of the 150 other cocktails on offer, while enjoying pop, disco, mainstream, chill-out and 90´s music in this atmospheric bar, with stylish restaurant and café. The rich interior décor in this interesting complex of large and cosy small rooms exudes the spirit of distant Brazil, complemented by excellent cof-fees, cigars and a discotheque, making it a great venue right in the centre. Hviezdoslavovo námestie 15, 🖼 2 CS 27

🔗 riorestaurant.sk

4 Beer Palace

In this truly historical beer palace just a skip away from the Opera, you can expect exactly what

is promised – excellent, fresh, non-pasteurised beer from copper tanks, tasty traditional regional cuisine and concerts in the evenings with various live acts. After a roast duck, some 'Halušky' gnocchi, or a game goulash, only empty plates remain. Gorkého 5, 🖼 2 CX 25

🔗 beerpalace.sk

5 Casa del Havana

A cocktail bar in an attractive place bringing to Bratislava a bit of Havana along with Cuban kinds of entertainment. Rooms decorated with various artefacts from Cuba, excellent Cuban cuisine, a large selection of cocktails and an irresistible atmosphere make this bar a favourite for Latino-style entertainment. On Wednesdays and Thursdays, courses of salsa and merengue are given and on Fridays everybody spins to the Music Night. Anyone who hasn't had enough can stay on for the Monday Party. Michalská 2, 🖼 2 CR 22

🔗 havanacafe.sk

6 Cafe Studio Club

A former recording studio now fitted out as a music club that offers various kinds of music just about every day. Jazz, blues, and swing live – everybody will find something to his liking

but must get there early enough - before 7 p.m. One of the best venues in the Old Town for this kind of music. During the day it functions as a coffeehouse with soft music.
Laurinská 13, 🔲 2 CZ 22

7 Nu Spirit Bar

In the course of the day, Nuspirit looks like a teahouse with a hippie atmosphere. The small cellar rooms are popular with students in the daytime and nu jazz enthusiasts at night. Every day except

Tuesdays the DJ plays various forms of jazz and live concerts are held here regularly. You come here to relax to the pleasant music. This Music club in the centre is open until the early hours.
Medená 16, 🔲 2 DB 26

🖱 nuspirit.sk

8 Moods

In the narrowest street in the city, a beer parlour that since time immemorial served for storing wines has welcomed them back after a lengthy absence. Moods is associated with excellent wines, original art and fine cuisine. It is an excellent combination that leaves you in a good mood, of course. The right choice for those who

want to sample a choice of fine Slovak wines. Baštová 3, 🔲 2 CQ 20

🖱 moods.sk

9 Music Bar Priatelia

Priatelia, or friends, is a unique concept for a music bar in the Old Town in an interesting functionalistic building from the turn of the 1920s and 30s. The interior is done in the style of the TV series Friends. Come along and dance with some friends to music from the good old 80's and 90's, pop, r'n'b, and also to live music concerts.
Hurbanovo nám 6, 🔲 2 CS 19

🖱 musicbarpriatelia.sk

10 Vínimka

After a long period of silence, wine bars are making a comeback. This time in a more sophisticated and modern form. Vínimku, a play on the words wine and exception, was opened by one of Slovakia's best known sommeliers, so no lack of excellent wines from all over the world here. The wines list includes some Slovak wines from less known winemakers, but also those from Slovakia's top producers. No problem either getting something small and tasty to eat.
Ventúrska 3, 🔲 2 CQ 26

Clubs

1 Nu Spirit Club

An excellent venue for entertainment, whether at a concert, discotheque or just sitting at the bar

enjoying the music. A rich events programme, interesting live music nights, various styles of dance parties, theme nights, and club talk-show evenings with various guest artists. Brazil party, Funk evening, Jazz night, Soul party, Hip-hop night, Electronic music night, and an excellent array of DJs, all with the atmosphere of a modern bar offering quality drinks and cocktails.This Music club in the centre is open until the early hours. Šafárikovo nám. 7, 🗺 2 DG 28

⌐ nuspirit.sk

2 Le Club by Medusa

Modern elegant venue with comfortable armchairs, stylish seating, uniquely designed bar and also original large and smaller private rooms on Hviezdoslavovo námestie. A good place to relax, have fun, dance, or meet up to enjoy a pleasant evening with music and a favourite drink. In the summer you can sample the club's atmosphere also outside on the terrace, which is enhanced by live plants and atmospheric lighting. Hviezdoslavovo nám. 25, 🗺 2 CU 26

⌐ leclub.sk

3 Trafo Music Club

The only club right in the city centre is concealed underground in an elegant palace. It did not get its name by accident; behind a wall of transparent glass there is an electricity transformer substation which supplies part of the Old Town with energy, setting it in motion exactly as Trafo energises the fun-seekers who are drawn here by the excellent music, light-show and latest designs. All that goes on is presided over by Mick Jagger in an original painting by Andy Warhol. Ventúrska 1, 🗺 2 CQ 27

⌐ trafo.sk

4 Carat Club

This exclusive night club is to be entered from the side of the Crowne Plaza Hotel. You will be excited not only by the luxurious interior and a computer-operated laser show but especially by the charming dancers showing off their skills on a catwalk. There are Sky Boxes available for those who are up for a Private Dance. Poštová, 🗺 2 CU 15

⌐ caratclub.eu

5 Olympic Casino

Olympic Casino in the Radisson Blu Carlton hotel is the most modern and only non-stop casino in Bratislava. You will be impressed by the elegantly designed interior with big bar. Exceptional added value is entertainment in the style of Las Vegas casinos. You can always find some live music, DJs, fashion shows or theme nights there. In this casino you will be pleased by 13 live tables (American Roulette, Black Jack, Oasis Poker, etc.) and 62 slot machines. Hviezdoslavovo námestie 3, 🗺 2 CU 28

⌐ olympic-casino.com

6 UFO Groove Club

It happens only once a month on a Saturday but there's no other place to compare with it. At a height of 85 m above the city on the pillar of the New Bridge, the entertainment is

an adventure in one. Its location, resident star DJs, superb cocktails and delicious sushi have made UFO an exceptional place which attracts

the young and successful. Due to its limited capacity of 150 people you have to plan ahead. Nový most, 🔲 2 CO 36

⌐ u-f-o.sk

7 Flamenco Music Club

There is nowhere better for lovers of Latin-American dance in Bratislava. At the weekend it's difficult to find a vacant space here. The pleasant environment and people, positive energy, a large selection of drinks and catchy atmosphere – it's hot here at night. Salsa courses offered by good-looking teachers attract a lot of girls.
Štefánikova 14, 🔲 2 CR 5

8 Harley Davidson

Harley Bar & Restaurant – spacious venue with rich programme of events, 5 bars, air-conditioning, restaurant, grill, large terrace, children's playground, problem-free parking and friendly staff in a Wild West come Mexican atmosphere. Regular discotheques and special

⌐ harley.sk

9 Primi

Comfortable seating over two floors, the largest year-round patio in the city, with garden armchairs, stylish furniture, large selection of meals and cocktails, always with excellent background music. Local DJs provide entertainment every Friday and Saturday, turning it into an excellent dance party through to the small hours of the morning. With a capacity for up to 250 people, it is the perfect venue for large private functions. Right next to St. Michael's Gate in the heart of the city centre,

you can enjoy the atmosphere of a truly modern establishment.
Michalská 19 – 21, 🔲 2 CR 20

⌐ primi.sk

10 Cafe Studio Club

A former recording studio now fitted out as a music club that offers various kinds of music just about every day. Jazz, blues, and swing live – everybody will find something to his liking but must get there early enough - before 7 p.m. One of the best venues in the Old Town for this kind of music. During the day it functions as a coffeehouse with soft music.
Laurinská 13, 🔲 2 CZ 22

Latino, Mexican, Beach, Red Bull and Jack Daniels – Black Jack theme evenings, as well as Reggae parties and other nights, all guarantee a great night out at this large venue.
Rebarborová č. 1/A, 🔲 3 AJ 9

Accommodation

Luxury Hotels

1 Sheraton***** €€€

The prestigious Sheraton hotel offers you top quality services, highly motivated staff and comfort all in one elegant package. The

hotel is located in the city centre on the embankment of the River Danube, as part of the modern Eurovea shopping complex. This is the first hotel of the company Starwood in Slovakia, containing 209 luxurious rooms, including 23 suites and 17 rooms with balconies or terraces giving spectacular views. The eye-catching interior design, interesting mix of colours and the wide range of services offered by Amber's Bar, the Brasserie Anjou restaurant and the Shine Spa centre, will make a strong impression on you and leave you feeling good.

Pribinova 12, 🔲 2 DK 29,
📞 +421 2 3535 0000

🖮 sheratonbratislava.sk

2 Kempinski Hotel River Park***** €€€€

A hotel that will satisfy even the most demanding guests. The luxury on offer at the Kempinski Hotel River Park was missing in Bratislava in

the past, but now on the bank of the River Danube, just a few minutes from the Old Town centre, you can find an excellent standard of service and style. The hotel has 231 luxurious rooms and suites on 11 floors. The top floor of the hotel features the Zion Spa & Health Club with an impressive view of the river. The modern building was designed by well-known Dutch architect Eric van Egeraat.

Dvořákovo nábrežie 6, 🔲 2 CE 31,
📞 +421 2 3223 8222

🖮 kempinski.com

3 Hotel Arcadia***** €€

A new addition to the top-ranking hotels in Bratislava is housed in a Mediaeval building known as Husites' House with stunning view of the Franciscan church from the 13th century. This boutique-hotel with a beautiful Renaissance atrium will satisfy everybody who is seeking antique surroundings matched with 21st century comfort. Despite its location in the Old Town there are no problems with parking as there is an underground carpark just a few metres away.

Františkánska 3, 🔲 2 CT 20,
📞 +421 2 5930 8585

🖮 arcadia-hotel.sk

4 Albrecht***** €€

If you feel like escaping from the city centre for a while and want to experience the comfort of a cosy boutique hotel, you should try the Albrecht Hotel. The hotel offers quality accommodation in twelve premium standard rooms in a historical building that has been renovated in an elegant, modern style. With beautiful interiors, a restaurant with a delicious menu, a conservatory and a terrace, it is the perfect venue for social gatherings or regular chillout and jazz evenings, guaranteeing a truly pleasant experience.

Mudroňova 82, 🔲 2 CC 25,
📞 +421 2 6720 0091

🖮 hotelalbrecht.com

5 Tulip House***** €€€

The Tulip House Boutique Hotel in Bratislava is a very interesting building, architecturally belonging to the Art Nouveau style of the Vienna Secession. The hotel also has spacious maisonette apartments located on the top floor, which take the names of flowers (Tulip Penthouse, Camelia Penthouse, and the Orchid and Rose Penthouse). The Tulip House Boutique Hotel, created above the historically famous Tulip Café, also boasts an excellent restaurant, fitness centre and the conserved Tulip Café.

Štúrova 10, 🔲 2 DB 25,
📞 +421 2 3217 1819

🖮 tuliphouse.sk

ℹ️ Weekday prices for a standard double room with breakfast in the high season, including all taxes. Most hotels offer weekend and seasonal reductions.	
€	EUR <140
€€	EUR 140-180
€€€	EUR 180-230
€€€€	EUR >230

Big Moments are Better when Shared

Sheraton Bratislava Hotel is a welcoming
5-star hotel located along the EUROVEA
boulevard, just 10 minutes' walking
from the historical city center. Enjoy our
spacious rooms with Sheraton Sweet
Sleeper® Beds, relax in the Shine Spa for
Sheraton™ – a full Health Club & Wellness
Center – or dine in Brasserie Anjou with
an open kitchen and a summer terrace
on the lively EUROVEA Central Square.
Feel the atmosphere and take a break
from the ordinary.

Pribinova 12
EUROVEA
81109 Bratislava
Slovakia

Book at sheratonbratislava.com or call +421 2 3535 0000

Premium Hotels

① Hotel Marrols***** €€€€

A relatively small hotel located near the Old Town is distinguished for its charm and harmonious classical style of the 1920s. Anyone searching for something more personal will be hard put to find anywhere better in the whole of Bratislava. The hotel's human scale, the staff's exemplary attitude, the attention to detail, the high-quality beds, the excellent restaurant, a special room for ladies and many more attributes were the reasons for this hotel's inclusion in the network of Small Luxury Hotels of the World.

Tobrucká 4, 🗺 2 DC 28,
📞 +421 2 5788 4600

⬡ hotelmarrols.sk

② Hotel Crowne Plaza**** €€€€

This entirely refurbished large hotel with an attractive location opposite the Presidential Palace returns to the ring with its combination of modern design and timeless elegance. This business-hotel has significantly reshuffled the Bratislava pack and its wide choice of facilities for conferences makes it one of the top hotels in the city. The high standard of the well-equipped rooms with comfortable beds, a large relaxation centre Fitness Plaza, a number of conference and meeting rooms of different sizes, and an excellent restaurant meet all the requirements of the business clientele which dominates here.

Hodžovo nám. 2, 🗺 2 CT 14,
📞 +421 2 5934 8111

⬡ crowneplaza.com

③ Austria Trend**** €€

Modern luxury hotel with a focus on design. The hotel has 199 tastefully furnished rooms in the Superior, Business, Executive and Junior Suite classes, providing accommodation right in the center of Bratislava. A private Executive club, extensive conference facilities, a restaurant, a café, a bar and a relaxation zone with a sauna, fitness centre and cardio-equipment are a guarantee of comfort and a great time at this hotel. The hotel also has its own parking and its excellent location in the city centre is a major advantage.

Vysoká 2A, 🗺 2 CU 14, 📞 +421 2 5277 5800

⬡ austria-trend.at

④ Falkensteiner**** €€€

The unique Falkensteiner hotel boasts the architecture and atmosphere of a modern lifestyle, a central location, top-class services, an excellent restaurant, a bar, and a fitness and relaxation centre. It is suitable for a business trip, romantic moments or for a longer stay in Bratislava. Guests receive a stylish welcome from the extravagant modern interior, conference rooms, Business Corner, Cigar Lounge and the hotel lobby, with top quality services.

Pilárikova ulica 5, 🗺 2 CN 19,
📞 +421 2 5923 6100

⬡ falkensteiner.com

⑤ Hotel Radisson SAS Carlton**** €€€€

No other hotel of this size in Bratislava can ever have a more attractive location than Carlton. It is situated right next door to the Opera House on the edge of the Old Town. It was founded at the beginning of the 20th century by the combination of three famous hotels of the time, each with a rich history. Following a complete reconstruction, and being enrolled within the Radisson SAS network, it successfully continues the traditions of its predecessors as a place for important meetings and a conference venue. From rooms furnished in the current fashion, through classical to the luxurious Maria Theresa room, there is something here to suit everyone's taste.

Hviezdoslavovo nám. 3, 🗺 2 CU 28,
📞 +421 2 5939 0000

⬡ radissonsas.com

6 Avance**** €€

Twenty six top-standard rooms, two super luxurious apartments and one presidential suite, a modern wellness center, conference rooms, private parking and the highest standard of services. These are all guaranteed at hotel Avance. In addition to the hotel's large selection of facilities, its location is also an advantage. Within walking distance from the hotel there is Hviezdoslavovo námestie, the old building of the Slovak National Theatre and the Main Square (Hlavné námestie).The hotel's luxurious restaurant offers specialities of international cuisine as well as traditional dishes.
Medená 9, 🔍 2 CX 29,
📞 +421 2 5920 8400

☞ hotelavance.sk

7 Gate 1**** €€

A place where elegance meets with the classics. This modern hotel with services of the highest quality is just minutes away from Bratislava Airport. The hotel offers accommodation in 121 elegantly furnished rooms. It also boasts a restaurant that serves European specialties, a relaxation center, a lobby bar, a pool, a Jacuzzi and a real feeling of comfort in a classy atmosphere. Make your business meetings or visit to Bratislava more pleasant with the services of Gate 1 hotel. Ambrušova ulica 7, 🔍 3 FM 6,
📞 +421 2 3277 0000

☞ gate-one.hotel.relaxos.sk

8 Hotel No. 16**** €€

For several years now, this bijou hotel owned by a famous couple of artists has been an oasis for people seeking something original and intimate. It is situated in a villa in a beautiful and quiet quarter near the Castle and it makes the most of its unique atmosphere in a minimum of space. Antique furniture, home comforts, spectacular views of the Castle, a beautiful garden and, with a bit of good fortune, you will be treated to a piano recital from your host, a famous Slovak pianist – all of this you can find at No. 16.
Partizánska 16a,
🔍 A2 CC 17,
📞 +421 2 5441 1672

☞ hotelno16.sk

9 Art Hotel William**** €

This new comfortable hotel is situated in an interesting building dating from the 1930's, located above what was Bratislava's first shopping mall called Central Passage. The sole drawback to its superb location in the Old Town is its relative distance from underground parking facilities for those who come to Bratislava by car. This relatively small hotel equipped in the latest Italian design has attracted a clientele who want to be where it is happening in Bratislava.
Laurinská 17, 🔍 2 CZ 22, 📞 +421 2 5988 9444

☞ euroagentur.com

10 Skaritz**** €€

At Skaritz hotel you can find romantic and impressive hotel and apartment accommodation directly in the pedestrian zone of the Old Town, in a renovated 600-year old building on Michalská ulica. Set out on three floors, with eleven double rooms, three suites and six apartments, the hotel provides quality accommodation and excellent food right in the city centre. All the rooms are non-smoking. You can also take advantage of the typical Slovak restaurant, a lounge, business centre, fitness gym, sauna, or revitalise yourself with a Thai massage.
Michalská 4, 🔍 2 CR 23,
📞 +421 2 5920 9770

☞ skaritz.com

ℹ️ Weekday prices for a standard double room with breakfast in the high season, including all taxes. Most hotels offer weekend and seasonal reductions.	
€	EUR <120
€€	EUR 120-140
€€€	EUR 140-170
€€€€	EUR >170

Mid-Range

1 Hotel Apollo**** €€

This completely reconstructed medium-sized hotel is situated in the wider city centre close to the bus station and the new business quarter. The original three-star hotel has had its interior totally transformed and, by dint of its attractive pricing policy, poses strong competition within its field. Those who do not need to be right in the city centre but still demand comfort have come to the right address. The appropriately equipped conference facility, the new relaxation centre and the best and largest hunters' restaurant in Bratislava (see p. 83) all have their regular clientele.

Dulovo nám. 1, 🔍 1 BJ 20, 📞 +421 2 5596 8922

🖱 apollohotel.sk

2 Hotel Ibis Centrum*** €€

A hotel belonging to a well-known chain, of medium capacity, immediately below the Castle and at the edge of the Old Town, occupies an ideal location from which everything important can be reached on foot. Ibis offers attractive prices and an established standard so nothing will surprise you. Those who do not mind an impersonal and simple style, are looking for something in the city centre and, despite its location, for a very good price don't need to think twice. Those who are light-sleepers or who do not want to be woken early in the morning should request rooms away from the tram-tracks.

Zámocká 38, 🔍 2 CL 22, 📞 +421 2 5929 2000

🖱 accorhotels.com

3 Mercure**** €€€€

Whether you are a business traveler or visitor to Bratislava, the quality services of this new hotel - a simple modern six-floor building a short walk away from the Main Railway Station, will definitely suit you. The hotel's elegant interior

and colourful accessories make it unique. Mercure offers plenty of comfort in its 175 uniquely furnished rooms. It also has conference facilities, a bar, a restaurant, a leisure center and its own parking. The hotel is part of the Accor Hotels network.

Žabotova 2, 🔍 1 AT 14, 📞 +421 2 5727 7000

🖱 mercure.com

4 Chopin*** €€

The Chopin Airport hotel is a good solution for travelers on a business trip. There are 174 comfortable modern rooms that are elegant and cosy, thanks to the predominant red and yellow combination. There are also six fully air-conditioned conference rooms with a total capacity of 320 persons, together with modern audiovisual equipment and plenty of daylight. Bratislava city centre is about 15 minutes away.

Galvaniho ul. 28, 🔍 3 FM 6, 📞 +421 2 3229 9100

🖱 chopinhotel.sk

5 Hotel Tatra**** €€

This is a recently completely refurbished city hotel of a medium size, with a long tradition, built at the beginning of the 1930s in the International Style. It has an excellent position in the centre of Bratislava near the Presidential Palace and close to the Old Town. Its location on a busy street in the city centre is ideal for those who want to be in the centre of events. Those whose need is for a quiet place to sleep should request rooms facing onto the garden of the Presidential Palace. Due to its good con-

ference facility and the cinema right in the building, the hotel is suited to company presentations and activities.

Nám. 1. mája 5, 🔲 2 CV 11,

📞 +421 2 5927 2111

🖱 hoteltatra.sk

6 Sorea Regia*** €

This medium-capacity hotel, 10 minutes from the city centre, is located in a quiet place surrounded by a lot of greenery on the hill above the Danube. There is a choice of several categories of practically equipped rooms with modern furniture. This place is ideal for people who are looking for accommodation near the city centre in a quiet surrounding, and who require a basic standard and a clean environment at a very competitive price.

Kráľovské údolie 6, 🔲 1 AH 25,

📞 +421 2 3211 2870

🖱 sorea.sk

7 President*** €

In the quiet historical centre of Bratislava, this hotel will welcome you with its inventiveness and simple modern design, offering a pleasant and friendly atmosphere and a high standard of services. The hotel has cosy rooms with standard European amenities. The hotel premises are suitable for business meetings, training courses, seminars, conferences, banquets or celebrations. There is also a presidential suite for VIP guests.

Drevená ulica 4, 🔲 2 CT 16,

📞 +421 2 5441 0522

🖱 presidenthotel.sk

8 Danubia Gate**** €€€

The Danube Gate hotel provides modern and comfortable accommodation in Bratislava city centre, as well as excellent technical equipment and free parking. The hotel interior, the rooms and meeting facilities are furnished in a luxurious and elegant style.The hotel has a capacity of 25 rooms, which include single, double and De Luxe rooms. One of the rooms is complete-

ly furnished for the convenience of disabled guests. The hotel has its own restaurant called the Street Coffee & Restaurant.

Dunajská 26, 🔲 2 DG 20, +421 2 2066 5500

🖱 hoteldanubiagate.sk

9 Hotel Matyšák*** €€€€

This newly-constructed, medium-sized hotel, close to the main railway station and the Old Town, has something that others can only envy. It is built on a hundred-year-old wine cellar which has become an attractive wine store and a venue for wine tasting. The wine cellar is connected with a top-quality wine restaurant (see p. 79). Behind all this is one of the country's leading wine-producers and he could not have made a better use of this place. The rooms and suites are of high-quality, furnished in a classical elegance; the hotel has facilities for smaller conferences and seminars.

Pražská 15, 🔲 1 AS 14, 📞 +421 2 2063 4001

🖱 hotelmatysak.sk

10 Michalská Brána*** €€€

A hotel that brings the past and the present together in a pleasant way. The hotel is in the city centre pedestrian zone in a quiet street, which is in fact the narrowest street in Bratislava. The Michalská Brána hotel is close to the majority of foreign embassies. The hotel offers 14 rooms - singles and doubles - and suites in various designs and sizes, with modern furnishing. Right next to the hotel is Michael's Gate, which is a remnant of the town's original fortifications.

Baštová 4 , 🔲 2 CP 21, 📞 +421 2 5930 7200

🖱 michalskabrana.sk

ℹ️ Weekday prices, including taxes, for a standard double room with breakfast in the high season. Most hotels offer substantial weekend and seasonal reductions.	
€	EUR <80
€€	EUR 80-100
€€€	EUR 100-120
€€€€	EUR >120

Small Hotels and Pensions

1 Old City Hotel €

This new tiny hotel with six rooms is located right under the roof of a historical building immediately in the heart of the Old Town. Cosy and comfortably furnished rooms under the roof. No lift, no access by car but right in the centre of events.

Michalská 2, 🗺 2 CR 21,
📞 +421 2 5443 0258

🖇 oldcityhotel.sk

2 Chez David €€

This lovely pension with eight rooms and a homely atmosphere is situated under the Castle just a stone's-throw from the city centre. Light rooms furnished in a modern style, a hospitable staff, excellent Jewish restaurant and its own car park.

Zámocká 13, 🗺 2 CL 21,
📞 +421 2 5441 3824

🖇 chezdavid.sk

3 Film Hotel*** €€€

A small theme-hotel where everything is focused on the celebrities of the cinema. Each of its thirteen well-equipped rooms is named after a famous actor. A good location on a quiet street in the city centre and good value for money.

Vysoká 27, 🗺 2 CZ 12,
📞 +421 2 5293 1600

🖇 filmhotel.sk

4 Pension Gremium €€

This pension is housed above the bar of the same name in the Old Town on the street behind the Opera House from where everything is readily accessible on foot. It has five rooms furnished in a modern style and a friendly and natural atmosphere.

Gorkého 11, 🗺 2 CZ 24,
📞 +421 2 2070 4874

🖇 penziongremium.sk

5 Hotel Arcus Garni*** €€€

A charming small family-hotel in a quiet street in the centre near the Medical Garden and bus station. As a result of the design of this building, built in the Cubist style in the 1920s, the rooms are spacious and light with high ceilings. Above-standard bathrooms.

Moskovská 5, 🗺 2 DM 6,
📞 +421 2 5557 2522

🖇 hotelarcus.sk

ℹ Prices, including taxes, for a night for two persons in a double room with breakfast.	
€	EUR <70
€€	EUR 70-90
€€€	EUR 90-120

Budget Hotels and Hostels

1 Possonium Hostel €€

A pleasant new hostel, favoured by its proximity to the main railway station. The Old Town where everything happens is only a 15 minute walk away. Rooms with 2, 4, 6, 8 or 10 beds are available. The hostel has internet and wifi free of charge, a fully equipped kitchen, washing machine and a pleasant terrace in the summer. It is not usual for a hostel to be provided with the kind of stylish brick-walled cellar bar that you can find in Possonium.

Šancová 20, 🗺 1 AU 15, 📞 +421 2 2072 0007

🖰 possonium.sk

2 Downtown Backpacker's Hostel €€

This is the most stylish of its kind in the whole of Bratislava. Backpacker's is located right in the centre near the Presidential Palace, in a small romantic historical building from where everything is readily accessible on foot. Its old-world interior and kindly staff all help to create an excellent atmosphere. There is a bar, kitchen, washing machine and 24-hour internet access. Backpacker's is a Hostelling International member.

Panenská 31, 🗺 2 CQ 13, 📞 +421 2 5464 1191

🖰 backpackers.sk

3 City Hostel €€

The newest hostel in Bratislava is housed in the quiet courtyard of a building on a busy shopping street in the city centre. In the immediate vicinity are a large number of bars, clubs and cafés. Simply and practically equipped 1-, 2- and 3-bedded rooms with individual toilets and shower are more like a budget hotel. A social room with TV and free of charge internet are provided. This hostel is not equipped with a washing machine or a kitchen.

Obchodná 38, 🗺 2 CX 15, 📞 +421 2 5263 6041

🖰 cityhostel.sk

4 Hotel Spirit €€€

There is no other building in the whole of Bratislava similar in appearance to this hotel. The avant-garde, even crazy, exterior makes a play with all colours and shapes and this is continued in the interior as well. It is located above the main railway station which is a good starting point to get to all the important places in the city. This hotel

offers accommodation in 1-, 2-, 3- and 4-bedded rooms and a dorm, all equipped with their own bathrooms. A lavish breakfast and internet are included.

Vančurova 1, 🗺 1 AT 4, 📞 +421 2 5477 7817

🖰 hotelspirit.sk

5 Hostel Blues €€

A new stylish hostel is situated right in the heart of Bratislava within easy reach of all life's necessities. Shops, sightseeing, restaurants and bars, clubs and cafés are all only minutes away. The staff make you feel at home, creating a friendly atmosphere and are ready to assist you as to where to go for entertainment and to enjoy your meal. The hostel has rooms with 2, 3 or 4 beds as well as dorms and even a roof apartment complete with terrace and a wonderful view. Hostel Blues has a fully-equipped kitchen with TV, an excellent bar, common room, free wifi, laundry, and baggage store.

Špitálska 2, 🗺 2 DE 16, 📞 +421 905 204 020

🖰 hostelblues.sk

ℹ Prices, including taxes, for a night for two persons in a 2-bedded room without breakfast.	
€	EUR <30
€€	EUR 30-50
€€€	EUR 50-70

Shopping & Beauty

Shopping Centres

1 Eurovea

The Eurovea complex has more to offer than just a traditional shopping centre. It is a multi-functional project that is unique not only in terms of Bratislava, but the whole of Central Europe. It boasts 150 shops and 30 cafés, bars and restaurants, and a tastefully landscaped Danube embankment with jetties and other architectural elements. A unique feature of the Eurovea Gallery is its glass roof. It is a great place for shopping, fun and relaxation on the

River Danube in the heart of Bratislava.
Pribinova 8, 🔲 2 DK 29

🔗 eurovea.com

2 Aupark

On the true-right bank of the Danube, next to the first public park in Central Europe, can be found Bratislava's most frequented shopping centre. It is the only one in the city which has succeeded in combining shopping with entertainment and wellness. You can find the current prestigious European fashion names, cinemas, specialist shops and services as well as the bowling and fitness centre. The centre is ideally suited for mothers

and children. There are a number of shops specialised in selling products for children and outside the centre there is a children's playground equipped with climbing frames.
Einsteinova 18, daily 10.00 - 21.00, 🔲 1 AT 35

🔗 aupark.sk

3 Polus City Center

Pleasant and compact in its architecture, this shopping centre is located within the area of greater Bratislava. With its hypermarket, a wide network of shops and 8 cinemas, it is a popular place for shopping and entertainment for Bratislava residents. A pleasant alternative to make shopping more interesting is to combine it with a visit to the neighbouring recreation resort on Kuchajda lake.
Vajnorská 100, daily 9.00 – 21.00, 🔲 1 BM 3

🔗 polus.sk

4 Avion Shopping Park

On the eastern edge of the city near the airport, alongside the motorway, the large Avion Shopping Park can be found. In addition to a standard hypermarket and a varied network of shops (H&M, C&A, Marks & Spencers, Peek & Cloppenburg), there is an artificial skating rink with the opportunity to attend skating classes and rent skates here. The high-quality services in this shopping centre are supplemented with a children's corner and a free shuttle bus running from Avion to Petržalka. This area is also provided with the IKEA, KIKA and HORNBACH D-I-Y stores. Ivánska cesta 16, daily 10.00 – 21.00, 🔲 3 FM 6

🔗 avion.sk

5 Shopping Palace

Near Avion is another shopping centre called Shopping Palace, designed in the Antique style. Its excellent location in the suburb of Bratislava near the recreation resort of Zlaté Piesky lake offers a unique opportunity for combining shopping, recreation and sports. Forming a part of this complex is the largest hypermarket in Slovakia open 24 hours a day. Shopping Palace offers a free of charge shuttle service running between New Bridge and Shopping Palace.
Studená 6, daily 10.00 – 21.00, 🔲 3 FM 4

🔗 shoppingpalace.sk

6 My Bratislava

Tesco is the biggest department store in the city centre. The original department store dating from the 1960s was reconstructed by the

British chain and offers shops and services to meet everyday needs. The department store is mainly used by city centre residents because it contains the only big supermarket

to be found in this part of the city. Kamenné nám. 1, Mon-Fri 8.00-22.00, Sat 8.00-20.00, Sun 9.00-20.00, 🔲 2 DC 21

⤳ itesco.sk

❼ Atrium

Interesting modern architecture and an excellent location on a main transport artery in the city has made Atrium a popular centre for design and stylish furniture and housewares. Shopping is made more interesting and entertaining by exhibitions and the view of the Bratislava Castle silhouette from behind the all-glass walls of the building.
Einsteinova street 9, daily 10.00 – 20.00, 🔲 1 AY 36

⤳ atrium.sk

❽ City Gate

A unique building that combines top quality accommodation with a luxurious shopping centre. In 2007, this seven-floor functionalist building, which was designed by the architects Eugen Kramár and Štefan Lukačovič in the 1940s, has been registered as a national cultural monument. The City Gate hotel represents a kind of gateway to the city and the link between

the old and new parts of the city. A comfortable shopping experience in a truly attractive environment. Námestie SNP 19, 🔲 2 DA 22

⤳ citygate.sk

❾ Central Passage

The premises of what was Bratislava's first shopping mall in a protected building dating from the 1930's, following a lavish reconstruction, now shine in their full beauty. At this prominent address, spread over two floors, you can find the latest hits in men's and women's fashions from famous designers such as Ferré, Armani, Gucii, Klein etc. On the upper floor there is a beauty salon and a hairdresser's.
Laurinská 17, daily 8.00 – 22.00, 🔲 2 CZ 22

❿ Tatra Centrum

With its very central position, this smaller-scale centre is housed in a modern bank building just opposite the Presidential Pal-

ace. Supermarket, cafés and restaurants as well as practical services such as laundry, florist, internet café, etc., are spread over two floors. The convenient parking in the underground garage is used not just by shoppers.
Hodžovo nám. 3, Mon-Fri 9-19, Sat 9-17, 🔲 2 CU 13

⤳ tatracentrum.sk

Markets

1 Christmas Market

Every year, on the Friday before the first Sunday in Advent, the lights are switched on on a Christmas tree erected on Main square and remain lit until the 23rd December which is the closing day for the Christmas Market. The unique atmosphere, the Christmas concerts on the square, mulled wine, punch, roast meat, pancakes known as lokše and cakes – all these serve to attract a growing number of visitors to Bratislava every year. The Bratislava Christmas Market is unique by way of their authenticity and traditional atmosphere which please every soul in the special period leading up to Christmas.
Hlavné nám., 🔍 2 CT 24

bratislava.sk

2 Crafts Markets

Two weeks before Easter, numerous stalls offer everything related to this tradition, especially decorated eggs. Then, from May to October, small wooden stalls selling handicrafts and artistic products and souvenirs from all over Slovakia are installed on the square. Picture postcards and guides as well as hand-decorated ceramic products, embroidered tablecloths, pictures and little items to remind you and your beloved of your visit to Bratislava.
Františkánske nám., 🔍 2 CT 22

3 The Old Market Hall

At the edge of the Old Town, close to the Primate's Palace, is found the Old Market Hall, constructed in 1910 and resembling a railway station. It functions as a market selling traditional fruit, vegetables and flowers and also local specialities – sheep's cheese, bryndza (a specially processed sheep's cheese) or typical Bratislava cumin bread can be bought in small shops on the ground and first floor. You can meet the locals of Bratislava who come here to have a quick, cheap lunch or to chat with friends over a cup of coffee or a glass of wine; quite simply, a picture of local colour.
Námestie SNP, 🔍 2 CY 21

4 Central Open Market

Everything here is fresh - scented and ripe home produce – fruit, vegetables, poultry, cheeses, funghi, spices or caravans selling fresh bread. Most people come here on Saturday when families buy fresh food for Sunday lunch. On that day, in addition to market sellers from Bratislava, those from South and West Slovakia arrive. In the general hubbub and shouts of the traders, the Slovak language mixes with Hungarian, the pleasant scent of fruit, fermented cabbage and funghi. The locals know that there's a wide variety of high-quality and fresh home-made products on offer here. This is still one of the few places where you can experience the true atmosphere of the old Bratislava.
Miletičova street, 🔍 3 FI 8

5 Market Hall

This is the biggest covered market where you can buy not only typical products such as fruit and vegetables, but also some specialities. On the first floor, a traditional shop with bio-dairy products is located offering home-made butter, goats' cheese, bryndza (a specially processed sheep's cheese), a large number of cheeses made from sheep or cow milk or curd cheese. At Christmas time this market is a popular place to buy carp and Christmas trees.
Trnavské mýto, 🔍 1 BF 13

Slovak Fashion

1 Velvet Galery

This is the top address of young Slovak fashion and design at affordable prices, offering also the chance to take away a unique easy-to-pack souvenir from Slovakia. Here you will find original pieces by Mária Stráneková (an intern of Alexander McQueen), Boris Hanečka, Lenka Sršňová, Martin Hrča and other young fashion artists, as well as great jewellery makers Beta Majerníková and Radka Kováčiková. As part of the Velvet project, you can visit the artists directly in their studios.
Hotel Crowne Plaza,
Hodžovo námestie 2, 🔲 2 CS 14,
📞 +421 910 544 999

2 Oľga Janderlová

A small shop with a family atmosphere on a busy street in the Old Town – these are the characteristics of Mrs. Jandelová's hat-shop. You can find a broad variety of classical and sports hats, caps, berets, gloves and accessories for ladies and gentlemen. The special charm of this place comes from the permanent presence of Mrs. Janderlová who advises, helps each customer to choose the best product or manufactures them to order.

The hat-shop of Mrs. Janderlová embodies everything that was always typical of shop-keepers in Bratislava –old-fashioned courtesy, personal service and expertise.
Laurinská 6,
🔲 2 CV 24

3 Vogel Couture

The exclusive Vogel Couture fashion atelier continues in the traditions of the predecessors of the current owner who were excellent dress-makers. Jana Kuzmová, a talented designer, is responsible for the atelier's creations; her credo is an excellent design for a particular type of woman, precise cut, high-quality and luxury material and a perfect finish. The atelier provides high-quality services and the highest elegance of haute couture. Over the course of several years, the studio has reached the top in Slovakia.
Nám. SNP 16, 🔲 2 DA 21

🔗 vogelcouture.com

4 Lea Fekete

A Slovak fashion designer, Lea Fekete is a constant in the Slovak fashion market who offers modes made from high-quality materials, modes of pure lines decorated with flowers or patterns. In the third millennium, she succeeds in using features of folk style lifted from the decorative character of folk costumes. Her work is supplemented with interior decoration or film costume design. In her shop in the courtyard in Segner House, you find not only beautiful dresses but also jewels, scarves, handbags and various other accessories.
Michalská 7, 🔲 2 CR 22

🔗 leafekete.com

5 Miklosko

A new boutique prêt-à-porter of the prestigious Slovak fashion designer Fero Mikloško is to be found in the courtyard of a palace on Laurinská street. An extensive range offers trendy ready-made clothes, original accessories and exclusive trinkets – all that with the unmistakeable imprint of their creator. Gowns, as the favourite part of his work, can be just one-off designs or can be custom-made.
Laurinská 3, 🔲 2 CV 24

🔗 miklosko.com

6 Richard Rozbora

A talented young Slovak designer, a graduate of a prestigious London fashion school, de-

signs beautiful and timeless creations subtlely underlining feminine beauty. He combines exquisite materials with exclusive laces in a refined finish. His models, on display in the new Couture Gallery in the centre of Bratislava, are not there solely to be admired.
Sedlárska 4, 🅠 2 CR 23

🔗 richardrozbora.com

7 Lydia Eckhardt

The grande dame of Slovak fashion design, who has acted successfully on this scene for several years, has her salon in an attractive place on the highest floor of a house opposite the Carlton Hotel. The name Lydia Eckhardt stands for exclusive ladies fashions for all age categories from models for everyday wear to social events. Every lady will be satisfied but adequate time needs to be reserved.
Hviezdoslavovo nám. 20, 🅠 2 CT 27
📞 +421 2 5443 2165

8 Donna Rosi

The fashion designer, Emília Harmathová, with her Donna Rosi fashion trade mark, has become one of the renowned salons specialising in ready-to-wear ladies' clothes in an elegant style stressing feminine lines. The shop on Dunajská street offers ready-to-wear models of suits, blouses, dresses for social events which can be fitted, and accessories. The salon on Kaštieľska street offers custom-made suits, gowns and wedding dresses made from high-quality materials in a variety of colours.
Shop - Dunajská 40, 🅠 2 DJ 19

Salon - Kaštieľska 15, 🅠 3 FL 9

🔗 donnarosi.sk

9 Twigi

At the edge of the Old Town is a pleasant shop with modes characterised by their sense of originality and creativity, made mostly from natural materials and designed by Zdenka Gundová whose style expresses a certain approach to life. In the shop next door, matching jewellery, silk scarves, hats, caps, wedding accessories or pictures or textile toys from Slovak painters and designers are available.
Klariská 7, 🅠 2 CO 21

🔗 twigi.sk

10 Dana Kleinert

Dana Kleinert's design studio is housed in a beautiful palace in the Old Town. It offers original clothing for ladies and men and accessories from her workshop made from high-quality materials and interesting design. Or, over a cup of coffee, get familiar with news from Dana Kleinert's interior design dominated by knitted ware with her typical "3D" effect. Expertise and styling are part of the service.
Panská 17, 🅠 2 CS 26

🔗 danakleinert.com

Something Original

1 Folk Folk

If you are looking for authentic folk art and typical Slovak souvenirs, this is one of the places to visit in Bratislava. You can find it right in Bratislava city centre next to the Main Square (Hlavné Námestie). On offer are beautiful wooden products, glass, porcelain, ceramic and metal products, embroideries, carpets, tablecloths, place mats, traditional folk costumes and clothing from different regions, paintings and musical instruments. Discover traditional Slovak folk art and culture all under one roof.

Rybarska brána 2 , 🔲 2 CT 24

2 In Vivo

In the courtyard of a Baroque palace, is a small magical shop offering handmade homeware designed by the two sisters who are the proprietors. Everything is from natural materials, there is an atmosphere of peace and a feeling of homeliness. Instantly, you are tempted to buy whatever you see. Candlesticks, wooden angels, decorative objects, photo-frames or cards from hand-made paper. Whatever you buy, you will please both your loved ones and yourself.

Panská ul.13, 🔲 2 CS 26

🔗 invivo.sk

3 Stylo Accessories

On a walk through the Old Town, on one of its main streets, there is a pleasant little shop selling original silver jewellery designed by a famous Slovak designer. Most of it is decorated with semi-precious and rare stones such as pearls, rock-quartz (crystal), rosy quartz or turquoise. Each item of jewellery is unique and

made in Slovakia. Their prices are pleasantly surprising as is the advice from a shop assistant who is familiar with every detail.

Michalská 4, 🔲 2 CR 22

4 Rona Glass

An excellent piece of advice for customers seeking high-quality transparent glass or just moderately decorated glass is to visit the shop of top Slovak glass producer, Rona, whose products attract the attention not only of traditional customers but also those looking for something modern or even designerware. Right there in the shop you can choose from a large variety of high-quality branded Slovak wines to fill the glasses your have just bought or a suitable candle for your new candlestick. The professional assistance and perfect service enhance in every customer a pleasant feeling from shopping.

Laurinská 6, 🔲 2 CV 24

🔗 rona.sk

5 ÚĽUV

If you are looking for something typical and of high quality from Slovakia, this is the right place. The network of ÚĽUV shops specialises in selling handmade traditional Slovak products from natural materials. The shops are supplied by artists from all over Slovakia. Blue and white printed textile material, wooden toys, linen tablecloths typical of the northern areas of Slovakia or folk musical instruments and Slovak

folk costumes. Certainly, what you buy here is something which cannot be found anywhere else.

Námestie SNP 12,
🔍 2 CZ 19
Obchodná 64,
🔍 2 DA 13

👉 uluv.sk

6 Art to Wear

Guarantees you something which is exclusively available here and is not to be had anywhere else. Art to Wear offers hand-painted handbags of a high artistic value. Make your choice from a variety of paintings, motifs and types of handbags and create your own style. From unobtrusive up to extravagant, there is a style to suit every taste, regardless of age. In addition to handbags, wallets or glasses cases and artistic jewel-cases are also available here.

Sedlárska 8, 🔍 2 CS 24

7 Bastion

The aim of this tiny shop in a former castle bastion is to display for foreign tourists a wide range of various traditional folk handicraft products whether decorative or for practical use and also wooden toys for children. Products from ceramics, wood, glass, and also paintings on glass, dolls made from dried maize leaves, embroideries, Easter eggs and tin soldiers can be found here.

Castle, 🔍 2 CG 27

8 Krištáľ Katka

The crystal shop Katka close to Saint Martin's Cathedral offers crystal glass products or crystal figures and chandeliers. The shop is popular with foreign visitors to Bratislava due to its excellent location, its variety of crystal, glass and ceramic products and its affordable prices.

Panská 24, 🔍 2 CQ 27

9 K Gallery

A small and inconspicuous gallery on one of the main streets of the Old Town offers the possibility to unveil the world of applied art and design which impresses with its originality. A permanent display of glass products by an important artist, Bořek Šípek, is on sale here. Many famous Slovak artists display their work in authors' exhibitions every month. This gallery is dedicated to those seeking something unique.

Ventúrska 8, 🔍 2 CR 25

10 Twigi

At the very edge of the Corso is a pleasant shop with a homely atmosphere where you will undoubtedly find something to appeal to you. Household items from photoframes to statuettes up to tablecloths and curtains arranged in apparent chaos will tempt you to rummage and to inspect every corner because what if there is just the right thing there that you have always been searching for? Most of the products are made in Slovakia or designed by the Twigi shop.

Klariská 7, 🔍 2 CO 21

👉 twigi.sk

Beauty & Wellness

1 Pierot Carlton

The beauty salon Pierot has several hairdressing salons of which the one based in the Carlton Hotel is in the most central location. Skilled hairdressers, pleasant surroundings, professional advice- all of this will add to your satisfaction. As well as hairdressing, the Pierot studio offers cosmetic services and nail design.

Hviezdoslavovo nám.3, daily 9.00 – 21.00,
🔍 2 CV 28

🖰 pierot.sk

2 Toni & Guy

One of the biggest hairdressing salons and, undoubtedly, providing the highest quality services in Bratislava, is located on SNP Square. Toni & Guy is an established network of London hairdressers' with a 40-year-old tradition. All the staff have undergone rigorous training and it is evident – its members are professional, kind and know what they're doing. Reservations are made by PC, thus maintaining records of who, when and what has

been done to your hair. Reservations need to be made sufficiently far in advance.
Námestie SNP 2, Mon 12.00 – 20.00,
Tues– Fri 10.00 – 20.00, Sat 9.00 – 17.00, 🔍 2 CT 18

🖰 toniandguy.sk

3 Studio Inzone

Inzoneis located in the underground premises of a historical house right in the heart of the city centre, near Main square. It provides all kinds of

services from cosmetics to manicures, hairdressing to pedicures. The pleasant staff and their professional attitude add to the pleasant feeling that you are doing something beneficial for yourself.
Rybárska brána 1, Mon-Sat 8.00 - 20.00,
🔍 2 CV 26

4 Sheraton/ Shine Spa

You will find yourself in a totally different world when you visit this relaxation centre. The beautiful and cosy atmosphere, abundant in pleasant fragrances, the nice staff, modern design, a play on colours and light - all combine to give the Sheraton hotel's Shine Spa a high standard of comfort. The centre ranks high thanks to specially selected materials and products such as massage, cosmetics and the personal care of every visitor. Refresh your mind and body and make yourself shine.
Pribinova 12, 🔍 2 DK 29

🖰 sheratonbratislava.sk

5 Darsana

The first ayurveda Indian massage centre is to be found in a picturesque house in a narrow little street in the Old Town. You will experience unique massages and procedures on authentic equipment using natural products imported from India. Also, the professionally trained and experienced practitioners come from the Indian state of Kerala, the home of ayurveda. The aim underlying these massages and procedures is the harmonisation of the life energies, the body, mind and soul.
Baštová 7, daily 10.00 - 22.00,
🔍 2 CP 21

🖰 darsana.sk

6 Studio Eternity

"To look good means to feel good." This sentence underpins the intention of the Studio Eternity. With its perfect location in the Old Town, this modern and excellently equipped centre offers the services of hairdressing, manicure, pedicure, cosmetics, massages with hot stones or hot chocolate, lympho-massages and mud-wrapping. Booking in advance is recommended but with a bit of luck you can get in without a reservation.
Michalská 16, Mon – Fri 9.00 – 21.00,

Sat 9.00 – 18.00, 🔲 2 CR 21

🔗 eternitystudio.sk

7 Les Palisades

Stylish surroundings in an excellent location, high-quality staff,
exclusive cosmetics –
this is the established
Les Palisades salon. As
soon as you enter you
will be looked after
from your head down
to your fingertips.
Hairdressing, cosmet-
ics, massages, man-
icure, pedicure – all
these services are provided using the highest quality preparations which underline
the quality of the final outcome.
Palisády 29, Mon-Fri: 9.00 – 20.00, 🔲 2 CI 14

🔗 lespalisades.sk

8 Relaxx

Seven days a week, 360 days a year, the largest
health centre in Bratislava offers a wide range
of fitness and relaxation activities, indoor golf,
as well as health and beauty care and nutrition-
al meals. It has a modern swimming pool, a gym,
a fitness centre, a relaxation centre, saunas and a
café. You will also love the excellent environment
with a beautiful view and lots of daylight. Trainers
and instructors are available.
Einsteinova 7, 🔲 2 CP 40

🔗 relaxx.sk

9 Sabai Thai Massage Center

In the underground rooms of a historical building
with a passageway, there is an oasis of peace and
quiet where your mind as well as your body will
feel relaxed. The exotic style of the interior is augmented by the pres-
ence of genuine Thais
performing massages.
Each type of massage
is aimed at a different
problem of your body
– a special massage for
the spine, for post-na-
tal women or for mas-
sages of the legs. Eve-
rybody will find here
what he/she needs.
Laurinská 4, daily 10.00 – 22.00, 🔲 2 CV 25

🔗 sabai.sk

10 Redivivo beauty institute

In the heart of the Old Town, awaits you the luxury Redivivo Beauty Institute in the smart Central
Passage shopping gallery. Here you will be treated in a very special way and they will create for
you something unique to make you look perfect.
You will be spoilt with the latest cosmetics and
given professional advice. Men are welcome just
like women. Under one roof you can have whatever service you may require - from hairdressing
through cosmetics up to medical cosmetics.
Laurinská 17, Mon - Sat 10.00 – 20.00,
🔲 2 CZ 22

🔗 redivivo.sk

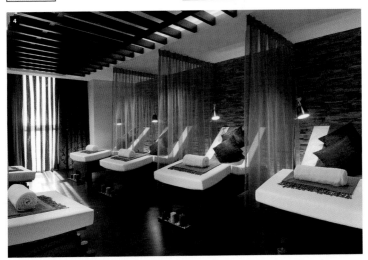

Antiques Shops

1 Soga Auction House

The only auction house of its kind in Bratislava offers landscape painting from the inter-war period, works of representatives of Slovak modern art of the 20th century, paintings from Central Europe from the 19th and the first half of the 20th century, European art from the period of the 17th to 19th centuries, sculpture and objects such as jewellery, porcelain or furniture. Auctions in Soga are held four times a year. The exhibits on offer are on display in a gallery.

Panská 4, 🔲 2 CS 26

🖱 soga.sk

2 Steiner

Steiner antiquarian booksellers has a long tradition of 150 years and it is a sine qua non part of the city. It specialises in books from the oldest periods up to current ones in various languages and also historical maps, drawings, lithographs and vedutas of towns and castles of the former Monarchy.

Ventúrska 22, 🔲 2 CR 23

3 Antik

In a palace courtyard, there is an impressive antiques shop whose goods are of two categories. The first category represents elegant period furniture with matching accessories or china. The second one offers historical rustic furniture, cupboards, clothes presses, kitchen furniture or ceramics mostly from the 19th century.

Michalská 3, 🔲 2 CR 22

4 Stanley Art

A tiny antiques shop where everything from carpets to chandeliers, from Renaissance to the 20th century, can be found. Apart from the genuine period furniture, historical weapons, china and glass are also on offer.

Ventúrska 14, 🔲 2 CR 24

5 Galéria Maráky

An antiques shop with a long family tradition dating from 1937, still located at the same address. Focused on art and antiques, furniture, pictures, plastic art and objects made from silver.

Panská 17, 🔲 2 CS 26

6 Margev Gallery & Antiques

A specialist antiques shop with old hand-woven Persian, Armenian and Turkish carpets. However, pictures, mainly from the period of Slovak and European modern art of the 20th century, naive art and jewellery can also be found here.

Palackého 14, 🔲 2 CZ 26

7 Secession

A small antiques shop specialising in the Art Nouveau period between 1890 and 1915 and Art Deco. Furniture as well as clocks, lamps, chandeliers, china, glass and utility objects from that period can be found here.

Palackého 8, 🔲 2 CY 28

8 Art Decoration

Probably the biggest antiques shop in the centre of Bratislava; in addition to the shop it has a gallery of its own. A part of its services is fur-

nishing interiors and the restoration of art objects, mainly furniture. Its depositories contain thousands of pieces of furniture and paintings from all over Central Eu-

rope. However, stoves, mirrors, china, glass and rarities can also be found here.
Kozia 15, 🔲 2 CL 17

⌲ artdecoration.sk

9 Still Art
An antiques shop aimed at the 20th century from the Art Deco period up to the present. On offer are mostly furniture and household items. The 18th and the 19th centuries are represented by furniture, pictures, sculptures and clocks.
Palackého 20, 🔲 2 CZ 26

🔟 Antiquariat Posoniensis
In the courtyard of an imposing building of the University of Fine Arts, a specialist antiquarian booksellers of a well-known Slovak restorer and a Berlin trader in period maps. Nowhere else can be found such a rich offering of historical maps and drawings of Bratislava and the territory of Slovakia. Everything sold here dates from a period before 1880.
Hviezdoslavovo nám. 18,
🔲 2 CT 27

⌲ posoniensis.sk

🖼 Art Galleries

1 Galéria Donner
A gallery with a large range of pictures, sculptures, graphic art, glass, jewellery as well as utility objects by well-known contemporary Slovak artists including those no longer alive.
Klobučnícka 4, 🔲 2 CY 21

2 K-Gallery
A small gallery filled with beautiful artistic and utility objects from glass by established Slovak artists. It also houses a permanent exhibition of works by Bořek Šípek.
Ventúrska 8, 🔲 2 CR 25

3 Galéria Nova
Eight times a year, the exhibits on sale of contemporary Slovak artists involved in the design and creation of objects from glass are renewed.
Baštová 2, 🔲 2 CR 20

⌲ galeria-nova.sk

4 ForZet Gallery
This gallery shows art-works by Slovak artists of the 20th and the 21st centuries.
Panenská 6, 🔲 2 CL 15

5 DIVYD Glass Gallery
This tiny gallery presents beautiful objects by top Slovak glass-makers of international renown, such as Ján Zoričák and many others.
Klobučnícka 2, 🔲 2 CY 21

⌲ divyd.sk

6 Galéria Brunovský
This small quaint gallery of a famous artistic family offers marvellous paintings, graphic and plastic art and jewellery by Daniel, Albín and Viera Brunovský.
Michalská 6, 🔲 2 CR 21

⌲ brunovsky.com

7 Galeria Medium
The gallery in the realm of the University of Fine Arts presents works by students, fine artists to be. An excellent opportunity for comparing their art with that of others.
Hviezdoslavovo nám. 18, 🔲 2 CS 27

⌲ vsvu.sk

8 Galéria X-style
A gallery of utility design with original ladies'clothing, jewellery, textiles and housewares – pictures, candlesticks etc.
Zámočnícka 5, 🔲 2 CS 20

9 Galéria Michalský dvor
In the palace courtyard is Art Shop offering the works of contemporary Slovak painters and graphic artists. In the adjacent cellar, a gallery with changing displays on sale is housed.
Michalská 3, 🔲 2 CR 22

⌲ gallery.sk

🔟 Kressling Gallery
This gallery displays the highest quality contemporary visual art from Slovakia and Central Europe. As well as presenting well-established artists, it also seeks out new talent.
Grösslingova 37, 🔲 2 DH 21

⌲ gallerykressling.sk

Walks & Trips

Discover the Charms of Bratislava

All the major sight-seeing venues in Bratislava are concentrated within its compact and attractive Old Town. The best place to begin a walking-tour is at the fountain in front of the Opera House. In the course of this tour you will discover the most beautiful squares of the city, narrow streets, elegant palaces, Renaissance courtyards, romantic corners, the most famous churches as well as the magnificent Castle and panoramic views over the city. If you are not in a hurry and want to see all the most noteworthy sights, some of them from the inside, and want to treat yourself to a short break in order to absorb all that you've seen, you should allow about half a day.

Approximately 3 km

Approximately 4 – 5 hours with breaks

Walking tours around the city and trips for groups:

msagency.sk 📞 +421 905 627 265

visit.bratislava.sk

---

1 Surroundings of the Opera House

The square in front of the Opera House is on the edge of the historical Old Town; it is a favourite meeting place for acquaintances, friends and lovers before they go for a cup of coffee, a stroll or for entertainment in the Old Town. It is also an ideal place for beginning a tour, as the visitor can follow a circuit and return to the same starting point. The **Opera House** (pp. 32-33) is a splendidly opulent building, a living symbol to Bratislava's rich musical traditions. The current building was constructed in 1884-86 to replace a former theatre built in 1776. Several years before that event, the town authority asked the queen for permission to pull down some of the town-fortifications (p. 41) which no longer served any purpose and were impeding the further development of the town. The town-walls were pulled down and replaced by the long row of houses still visible today. Also at this time, the branch of the Danube running by the town-walls was blocked off, giving rise to a long promenade with a small park in front of the Opera House. The former islands in the Danube disappeared and the land was developed. On the site of what is now the **Carlton Hotel** (p. 92) at that time stood some well-known inns, later converted into three hotels. They were joined together and redeveloped in 1925, thus resulting in the biggest and most modern hotel in the whole of the country. Next to it, there is another elegant building which was erected in 1913-1919 on the site of an old granary. This is **Reduta** (pp. 40, 58, 62), which since then has served as a place where concerts and spectacular social events take place. Here, the grandest of all the balls in the city are held each year during the ball season. Reduta is also the seat of the Slo-

vak Philharmonic, with the most imposing concert hall in the city.

1 Opera House – 2 "Čumil"

The Old Town is entered through **Rybárska brána** (Fishermen's Gate) situated next to the current narrow street. It was erected in the 15th century as the last of the four original gates in the town fortifications and demolished along with the town-walls in the 18th century. The lower part of the gate can still be seen beneath the glass canopy in front of the Opera House. Continue along the street towards the city centre and you can't fail to spot the statue of a helmeted man looking out of a drain. There are endless jokes and urban myths in circulation about him. His name is **"Čumil"** (the Watcher, p. 50) and, despite the fact that he does not represent any historical figure, he is the most frequently photographed subject in the city. Further on, there is the statue of a man with a top hat. **Schöne Náci** (p. 50) was an actual person (his name was Ignác Lamár) familiar to nearly all of Bratislava's inhabitants. He was a unique and amiable eccentric living in his own generous world. When he went strolling along the "Corso" he put on his only tuxedo, wore a top-hat and carried a cane. He greeted the ladies with a bow but when he thought a lady to be especially pretty he expressed his admiration with the German word "schöne" - hence his nickname. He died in the 1960s.

2 "Čumil" – 3 Main Square

Beyond the statue of Schöne Náci you pass **Kaffee Mayer** (p. 76) the most famous café in Bratislava established in 1873, a place that Schöne Náci himself liked to patronise. It's easy to understand why; once inside you will be struck by the huge variety of home-made cakes and tarts and the overall pleasant atmosphere of this place. If it's really too early for a break but at the same time you can't resist the attractions on offer, we suggest that you buy a traditional speciality of this city – **Pressburger Beugel** (p. 77) with walnut or poppy seed filling. Take it with you and enjoy the architecture and the speciality together. From the café you can see the square it overlooks – Hlavné námestie (The Main Square, pp. 26-27) which for centuries has been the heart of the city. In the Middle Ages this was the place where the most important markets in the town took place and still today the summer market for souvenirs and the traditional winter Christmas Market (p. 59) are held here. On the western side of the square stands the beautiful Art Nouveau building of a bank dating from 1904 (p. 27). Today, the original banking hall houses **Roland Caffé** (p. 76) with the Art-Nouveau mosaics preserved on the columns. The original strongroom serves as the kitchen. Even before you enter, the spectacular copper door decorated with Art Nouveau motifs will surely catch your eye.

In the centre of the square stands the oldest surviving fountain in the city, **Maximilian Fountain** (pp. 44, 46) dating from 1572. It is a popular place for locals and visitors alike to meet and rest and is named after the first king to be crowned in Bratislava – Maximilian II Habsburg. This is the small man in armour on the top of the fountain. The central part of the fountain is decorated with a column and statues of boys with fish. Originally there were four naked urinating boys but, following reconstruction in 1794, as shown on the plate below, the boys were replaced with less provocative statues. This part of the original fountain was rediscovered by chance in the 20th century and now forms part of another fountain in a courtyard of Ruttkay Palace (p. 46).

3 Main Square -
4 Primate's Palace

When you stand in the centre of the square and look around you, you notice that each building is completely different, originating from a different period, built in a different style and decorated in a different colour. Here, in this square, you could study architecture; all the styles from the 14th to the 20th centuries have their exponents here. The Square is dominated by the unique complex of buildings of the **Old Town Hall** (pp. 28-29). The individual houses to the right of the tower were gradually bought up, resulting in an extensive complex comprising buildings of various styles. Furthest from the tower, there is the Rococo-style Apponyi Palace, the courtyard of which (p.44) is one of the typical romantic corners of the old Bratislava. Two old wine presses are sited in the courtyard as symbols of the viticultural tradition of the city. In the past, presses like these stood in many courtyards as the majority of Bratislava's inhabitants were either wine producers or wine traders. The courtyard also houses one of the smallest but also one of the most beautiful cafés in the city, certainly worth a visit (p. 76). When you return to the square through the prized Gothic-style archway of the Old Town

Hall, be sure to take a look at its vault which is decorated with several interesting images of faces and coats of arms. The Old Town Hall courtyard is one of the most beautiful places in the city and is in constant use throughout the year; concerts, handicrafts markets, theatrical performances, wine tasting and many other activities are held here. The courtyard is a mix of various styles but harmoniously complementary. The overwhelming impression is evocative of the southernmost parts of Europe. From here, you can enter the **Bratislava City Museum** (p. 60) which is very interesting in itself and from here also you can climb the tower, affording the most spectacular views over the Old Town and the Castle. Beyond the courtyard you enter another small square. In order to have a better, overall perspective, stand on the steps of the building opposite the palace. From here, you can admire not only the Primate's Palace in all its beauty but also the rear part of the Old Town Hall which you have just left. You will be impressed not only by its Neo-Gothic façade but also by its colourfully glazed roof tiles.

4 Primate's Palace –
5 Franciscan Church

The Primate's Palace (pp. 22-25) is the biggest and best preserved palace in the Old Town and it serves at present as the Town Hall. Several events of historical significance have taken place here and it is one of the most important sights of the city The first floor is open to the public and if you have half an hour free you should certainly not miss its splendid interiors which contain the precious English royal tapestries. Continue through the courtyard of the palace where you will be impressed by the Renaissance St. George's Fountain. Then continue to the next courtyard and, if it is before 5 p.m. on a working day, turn left and via a small gate you get to a captivating courtyard in the Renaissance style (pp. 46-47) with the amusing fountain with the statues of the four urinating boys which were originally installed on the Main Square as part of the Maximilian Fountain. Notice that two of them are holding hands. Was this the reason for their removal?

Notice the sun-dial painted on the wall of the house. What you see is its morning part. Its afternoon part is hidden behind a window in a corridor of the opposite wing which was built later. (If the iron gate to the courtyard is locked, return to the front of the palace and rejoin the route by following Uršulínska street). Through the main entrance, you come out onto Uršulínska street, turn left and continue straight ahead to the **Franciscan Church** and its **Monastery** (pp.

30-31). From here, at the back of the church, the view of its Gothic tower is most picturesque. What is now a small park was, in the past, a famous Franciscan garden. Walk alongside the garden fence, turn to the left, and you will pass by a beautiful chapel in the Gothic style, dedicated to Saint John the Evangelist. It is one of the best preserved Gothic sights in the city. The Franciscan Church is the oldest in the city, has a rich eventful history and is worth a visit. The door to the right behind the entrance leads to the cloisters and courtyard of the monastery; it is of great note but is not always open.

5 Franciscan Church -
6 Trinitarian Church

Opposite the church entrance stands the most beautiful palace built in the Rococo style – **Mirbach Palace** (p. 41). Nowadays the palace forms a part of the Bratislava City Gallery (p. 60). It is positioned on an irregularly shaped plot of land and as a consequence its courtyard is outside the axis of the palace. This meant that the gateway would not have been in the centre of the building, spoiling the symmetry of the façade. Hence, the architect designed another gateway which is blind. The tour continues through a tiny narrow street on the right with a number of art galleries and students' haunts. One of them is just on the right, in a former bastion of the town-fortifications (p. 84). Its garden in the former moat is an ideal place for couples to spend romantic moments on hot summer nights. In the past, the houses in the small streets along the town-walls were mostly occupied by craftsmen. This one is named after locksmiths – Zámočnícka street. It leads into Michalská street directly at **St. Michael's Gate** (pp. 34-35). This is the sole surviving gate of the town-fortifications. Turn right and through the gate enter the so-called barbican which served as a defence for the gate itself. On the right is one of two remaining historical pharmacies in the city – The Red Crayfish. If it is open, have a look around - it will transport you back several centuries. Through the gate next door you can enter the former town moat (p. 49) which seems like an oasis of greenery and peace in the Old Town. Now at least, you will understand what this city is about and why those who have come to know it intimately love it so much. If you continue through the gate you get to the bridge across the moat. Opposite you is a modern-looking department store (p. 52) which is not nearly as new at it looks. In fact, it is a historical building, built in 1930. The square you enter is dominated by the Baroque-style Trinitarian Church (p. 42) with the most beautiful and best-preserved interior in Bratislava. Its large cupola with its trompe l'oeil fresco is unique in the whole of Bratislava. The church is only open during religious services; at other times you can admire its interior through the glass. From this spot, there is a pleasant view of the Castle (pp.14 – 17) and also the **Presidential Palace** (p. 40) where Joseph Haydn gave his concerts (pp. 64-65). In the distance, you can catch a glimpse of the vineyards which start right in the city itself.

6 Trinitarian Church -
7 St. Martin's Cathedral

Return to St. Michael's Gate. Just in front of the gate is the narrowest house in the whole of the city which is only as wide as the width of its door. The great gate next door leads to another niche in the former moat. After the gate, the narrowest street in the city - Baštová (Bastion) is located with its typical vaults supporting the houses

opposite. Originally this street was named Hangman's after the town hangman who lived in the third house on the left. Today, this is home to the office of a reputable dentist. Continue downhill along Michalská street which in summer is lined with terraces of restaurants. Don't omit to look both right and left for nearly each house has its own lovely courtyard (pp. 44-45) concealing a number of little shops, galleries, antiquaries, etc. If you also look down at your feet you will see the brass crowns symbolising the coronation route (p. 68). On your right you will see the imposing building of the **University Library** with a rich history (p. 40). Through the passageway in the building you get to another street with a former nunnery of Clare nuns which was later transformed into a secondary school where two well-known Hungarian composers **Béla Bartók** and **Ernst von Dohnányi** (pp. 64-65) studied. A short stroll uphill along the street will lead you to

the Eszterházy Palace which is still awaiting restoration. The palace was often visited by **Joseph Haydn** (pp. 64-65) who gave several concerts here. Return to Michalská street and continue to the right along Ventúrska street which is also noted for the fact that other renowned composers acted or gave their concerts here. On your right you will pass by the elegant de Pauli Palace (p. 40) where at the age of nine **Franz Liszt** (pp. 64-65) gave his first public concert. The next building is Zichy Palace where a predecessor and a rival of Richard Wagner – the German opera composer **Heinrich Marschner** (pp. 64-65) – was a music teacher. Be curious and peep into the courtyards on the right side of the street - you will not be disappointed. On the left you will pass by Palffy Palace, today housing the Austrian Embassy, where **W. A. Mozart** gave a concert at the age of six (pp. 64-65). Several metres further on the opposite side of the street stands **Academia**

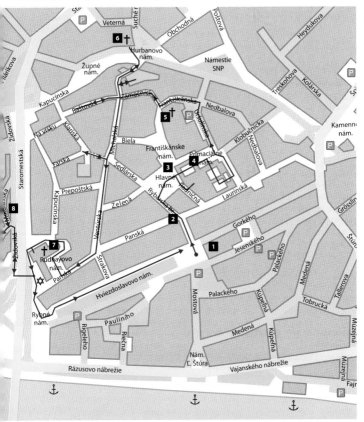

Istropolitana, the building of the first university on the Slovak territory, founded in 1465. At the crossroads, turn to the right. The smaller palace you will pass by is called Keglevich Palace, today the seat of the Danish Embassy. **Ludwig van Beethoven** (pp. 64-65) gave a concert here and acted as music teacher to a daughter of the owner of the palace.

7 St. Martin's Cathedral –
8 House of the Good Shepherd

Continue straight on till you enter a small square overlooking **St. Martin's Cathedral** (pp.18-21). Walk towards it following the broad steps behind a big tree and go around the cathedral from the back. The entrance to the cathedral is situated unusually on the north side because its west side formed a part of the town fortifications. Opposite its entrance there is a vestige of the municipal fortifications from the 15th century (p. 41). If the cathedral is open (p. 18) you will be highly impressed by the tour. The former coronation church of the Hungarian kings is one of the dominant highlights and most valued sights of the city. Outside again, keep walking to the left around the cathedral and follow the steps down to a small square. In the past, the biggest synagogue in the city was located here, but was demolished in the course of the construction of the New Bridge (p.54) which was built at the end of the 60s. Its location in close proximity to the biggest Catholic church symbolised the cosmopolitan character of the city and the coexistence of various national and ethnic groups. The place where it stood is now occupied by an expressive **Holocaust Memorial**. The synagogue is depicted on the marble wall. Turn and pass under the bridge and climb up the steps. The houses you see here are the only ones remaining of the entire, largely Jewish, quarter which was demolished at the end of the 1960s during the building of the bridge and its access roads. Continue to the **House of the Good Shepherd** (p. 40) which is so narrow that it has just one room on each floor. It is one of the most interesting houses in the whole of Bratislava. From this point there is a spectacular view of St. Martin's Cathedral as well as of the whole of the surviving fortification.

8 House of the Good Shepherd –
9 Castle

Continue to the left and climb steeply up Beblavý's street towards the **Sigismund Gate** of the Castle. This is the oldest gate leading to the Castle, constructed in the 15th century. Go around it to the left and continue along the fortification walls up to the modern building of the Parliament. Mount the broad steps leading onto the terrace of the Parliament and pass by flag-poles to the viewpoint overlooking the Danube. From this spot you can see a part of Bratislava, the fields and hills in Austria on one side and the whole Castle complex on the opposite side. Descend the steps and enter the Castle area (p. 14-17) through the Baroque-style **Vienna Gate**. Go up an ancient avenue. On the left there is a former summer riding school with a courtyard. The Castle tower visible from here originates from the 13th century and is the oldest part of the Castle. For centuries, the Hungarian royal crown jewels were kept here, which is why it is named the **Crown Tower**. Via the Victory Gate you will come to the southern terrace in front of the main entrance to the Castle. The Castle houses some very interesting museums which are entered via the courtyard. From the southern terrace, continue next to another Victory Gate down the steps to the Eastern terrace with a little park. You will be rewarded with the most spectacular view not only of the Old Town but also of the whole of the Bratislava city centre and the Small Carpathians with vineyards. Pass by a low building, a former stable-block and behind it descend the steps through the Castle wall out of the Castle area.

9 Castle – 1 Opera House

Go to the right down the steps passing a tiny church from the 17th century dedicated to St. Nicolas. You will get to the House of Good Shepherd again and return to the place of the Jewish memorial. Going towards the Danube you will get to **Rybné námestie** (the Fish Square). Up to the 1950s, fish markets were held here. The **Plague Column** dating from 1713 is erected in the middle of the square to commemorate the victims of the plague which killed about a third of the inhabitants of Bratislava. To the left is a long promenade lined with avenues of trees which is a popular resting place for locals and visitors to the city alike (p. 49). At its beginning, a statue of Hans Christian Andersen is displayed, surrounded with characters from his fairy-tales. He visited the city in 1841 and expressed a hope that the city would sometime remember the visit of this stranger. This hope has recently become a reality. Further along on the left there is the longest fountain (p. 46) in the city symbolising the former moat which ran here up to the 18th century. It finishes at the statue of one of the greatest of Slovak writers, Pavol Ország Hviezdoslav (p. 51). At the top end of the long square you will see the building of the Opera House where our tour began.

Danube, Bicycles etc.

In Bratislava you are never very far away from water. The Danube flowing through the city supplies Bratislava with high quality drinking water and has also created the marvellous floodplains, with a high level of ground-water. Thanks to it, a large number of semi-natural swimming pools have been created on the sites of former gravel pits. The well-known Danube cycle path follows the course of the Danube, starting in Austria and continuing through Bratislava down to Budapest. It is a very popular venue for sports-loving Bratislavans who wheel off after work in large numbers, on bikes or in-line skates, in a southerly direction towards the villages of Rusovce and Čunovo. These villages are surrounded with extensive floodplains with cycle-paths, lakes with crystal-clear water, a popular nudist beach as well as the romantic chateau with a large park, a shepherd's cottage with sheep, a purpose-built white-water sports area and a unique museum of modern art. And all this still within the city limits of Bratislava.

🚴	10 kms to Rusovce, 16 kms to Čunovo
🕐 🚶	Rusovce 1 hour, Čunovo 2 hours
🕐 🚲	Rusovce 45 mins, Čunovo 1 hour
🕐 🚗	15-20 mins
🕐 🚌	20-30 mins
ℹ️	Recommended map: VKÚ Harmanec, Malé Karpaty - Bratislava, 1:50 000, No. 127
🛶	rafting: ➥ raftovanie.sk
🖼️	gallery: ➥ danubiana.sk

If you are planning a bike or in-line trip, you can start in the Old Town and cross the river via the New or the Old Bridge to get to the true-right bank of the Danube. You can drive to Rusovce or Čunovo by car or take the 91 bus departing from the stop under the New Bridge on the true-left bank of the Danube.

The park (see p. 48) stretching between these bridges is one of the oldest public parks in Europe and it is worth having a look at it on your way. The cycle-path continues under the Old Bridge and further on under the Apollo and Port Bridges. The tarmac path follows the anti-flood embankment which is surrounded by floodplain forests, boating centres and gardens. After the last bridge, the view opens out and you can see wide meadows and the horse-riding club on the right. At frequent intervals there are rows of buffets and refreshment facilities offering drinks and a little something to eat. Further from the city large cornfields spread into the distance. The path leads by the seepage-water canal. Close to Rusovce, restaurants with spacious terraces wait for thirsty and exhausted sportsmen who congregate here and apparently have no plans to continue any further. This part of the cycle path is so popular and hence so busy, even overcrowded, that you have the impression you are on a motorway. Turning left behind the restaurants leads to a nearby branch of the Danube where a large number of houseboats are moored. There

is an option to descend to the right and join a broader road parallel with the seepage canal a few metres lower down. On the right, there is a large lake surrounded by woodland. Those who are only moderately energetic and want to rest, or those for whom this was their intended destination stop here and go swimming in the transparent waters of the Rusovce lake. Those who feel at ease about it take off all their clothes and enjoy this unofficial Bratislava nudist beach. The cycle-path continues along the wide road down to the dam and the water-sports area in Čunovo. This place is noted for its white-water competitions and provides rafting, suited even for beginners. Nearby, situated on a long peninsula, Danubiana, the attractive museum of modern art, presents its silhouette of a Roman galley in the distance (p. 60). These are attractions worth visiting by car if you are not provided with a bike. If you are enthusiasts of biking for pleasure and are not in a hurry, then do not return to the tarmac road from the lake but continue along the lake on paths in forests which will lead you through the ancient floodplain forests with old branches of the Danube and clearings and meadows. Do not be surprised if you meet a flock of sheep on your way, there is a large meadow in the forest with a tiny farm in the middle nearby. If you keep right and continue to the west you will cross an old channel via a small bridge and find yourself in a wide park with huge old trees surrounding the chateau in Rusovce. The glimpses of the romantic chateau in Tudor-Gothic style will make you feel as if somewhere in Great Britain. If you get hungry during your trip, there are several good restaurants in Rusovce which will help you regain your lost strength. Next to the chateau there is the SĽUK restaurant and a few hundred metres further, by the church, a romantic courtyard with Antica Toscana restaurant. In the middle of the village are several places where you can have baked fish.

Devín Castle and its Surroundings

For the local people, the western part of Bratislava is one of the most popular venues for a trip. Just 10 km west of the city centre, Devín Castle (see pp. 36-37) is set in beautiful natural scenery. Built on the top of a high crag, it towers over the small village of Devín and the confluence of the Danube and the Morava rivers which form the border with Austria. Up to 1989 the Iron Curtain was drawn below the Castle, lined with barbed wire. Along the Danube, under the Castle and further up the Morava, the Morava cycle-path leads through landscapes untouched for decades. Above the village of Devín, the highest hill of Bratislava is criss-crossed with a number of way-marked paths which offer spectacular views of neighbouring Austria with Vienna and the Alps in the background.

🏃 10 km

🕐 🚲 30-45 min (the path along the Danube starting under the New Bridge-Nový most)

🕐 🚗 15 min

🕐 🚌 20 min (No. 29 under the New Bridge- Nový most stop)

ℹ️ Recommended map: VKÚ Harmanec, Malé Karpaty - Bratislava, 1:50 000, No. 127
Canoe trip: 🛶 paddler.sk

There are actually two castles in Bratislava. Paradoxically, both of them were destroyed within the same two year period. While Bratislava Castle was rebuilt, Devín has remained a romantic ruin. However, this has not diminished its attractions; quite the opposite, since it is the most-visited sightseeing venue in the whole of Slovakia. It is also one of the largest castles in the country and is easily accessible from the centre of Bratislava by car, bus or bike.

The bus terminus is at a large car-park below the Castle; this is also a convenient place for car-parking. The Castle is entered via the gate situated behind the Castle Gate Hotel. The effort expended in climbing up to the central part of the Castle will be rewarded with a picturesque view of the surrounding landscape. You can try out the depth of the castle well by pouring water from a bucket. However, you have still more to do to deserve the spectacular panoramic views from the Upper Castle. A long, seemingly endless flight of steep steps awaits you. Once you get to the viewpoint and are hit by a powerful gust of wind, you will feel as though you're flying high above the land, like the hawk passing nearby. You are standing on the top of an 80-metre-high rock outcrop and you should add at least three more floors to it; such was the height of the Upper Castle. No wonder so many battles were fought over this place. In good weather conditions you can see Vienna and the peak of Schneeberg (2075 m) in the Alps. On your way down, a small path to the right behind the Middle Castle will lead you up to a grassy knoll (see p. 37) with the ruined foundations of a church from the 9th century. It's hard to imagine a place better suited to meditation. Back at the car-park, turn left.

The road leads you to the confluence of the Danube and the Morava.

All the land across the water, whether the Danube or the Morava, is Austria. It is just a stone's-throw away but for forty years it was an unattainable distance. Here was the barbed wire fence and many people were shot dead. Their unnecessary deaths are commemorated in a memorial bearing the names of the victims. In the meantime, if you have become hungry, return to the car-park and you can choose between the elegant hotel or a more folk-style restaurant offering specialities like roast knuckle of pork or beef goulash.

Those of you with bikes or in-line skates can continue along the Morava. The present cycle-path is the former military patrol route from which soldiers guarded the Iron Curtain. Because it was a long-term exclusion zone, the whole area along the river has retained its original habitat with its precious floodplain forests and water meadows which are home to beavers. Hikers can explore the western hillside of Devinska Kobyla (514 m), a nature reserve rich in precious and rare flora. In spring and summer, the meadows are dotted with beautiful flowers. The upper end of the car-park marks the start of a blue way-marked path which leads you out of the village. After a thirty-minute climb you are on the path, parallel with the Morava, leading to the Sandberg hill. The meadows are decorated with flowers, interspersed with occasional woodland, and you may find it difficult to concentrate on the path, so fascinating are the views of the Morava and Austria beyond the river. After another half hour's walk, sand cliffs open out in front of you. Millions of years ago, this was the shore of an ocean and if you look carefully you will see fossils of mussels in the sand. The path will lead you to the historical part of the village of Devínska Nová Ves. Turning to the left will lead you back to the Morava and the main road. You can return to Devín by bus or walk along the Morava. Those who would like to explore this unspoilt stretch of river with paddles in their hands, and observe storks and herons on the way, should start a raft trip in the village of Vysoká pri Morave and finish beneath the Castle. A raft trip like this lasts the whole day.

Bratislava's Forests

There are probably not many European capitals with woodland and dense forests reaching right into the city centre. Here in Bratislava, it is the hills of the Small Carpathians which are readily and quickly accessible by car, bus or bicycle. This adds to the quality of life for Bratislavans and they make use of it with pleasure for recreation or sports activities. Among the most popular places are the valley of the Vydrica stream, several km long, called Železná studnička (Iron Well) and the hill of Kamzík with its TV tower towering close over the city. Due to the forests, despite the small distances involved, Bratislava has two distinct climatic zones. The difference in temperature between the forests in the northern part of Bratislava and the Pannonian lowlands in the south can reach several degrees Celsius.

🚶 5 km	Bridge) stop to Patrónka stop; change to 43 bus from Patrónka to Železná studnička (Iron Well), 20-30 min	🪑 The valley up to the chair-lift: 4 km
🕐🚶 1 hod		ℹ️ Recommended map: VKÚ Harmanec, Malé Karpaty Juh, 1:25 000, n°9
🕐 45 mn	By trolley-bus: No. 203 from the stop at Hodža's Square (opposite the Presidential Palace), 10 min	
🕐🚲 30 min		📷 lanoland.sk
🕐🚗 From the city centre 10 min		shoppa.sk
🕐🚌 By bus: No. 30 or 37 from under the Nový most (New		altitude.sk

This trip can be started from either end - Železná studnička or Kamzík (440 m). For Železná studnička you can take a bus, for Kamzík a trolley-bus followed by a pleasant half hour's walk (1.5 km). By car it takes 10 minutes from the centre to both places. The valley of the Vydrica stream was well-known to millers as early as the Middle Ages and there were nine water-driven mills here. In the 18th century, springs of water with a high iron content were discovered (the name Železná studnička - Iron Well derives from them) on this site and a small spa building was erected which was replaced by a new, more elegant building at the beginning of the 19th century. Even at that time, this place was popular with the inhabitants of Bratislava and, after construction of the railway from Vienna, a large number of Viennese made trips here or came for cures in the spa. In summer, hikers enjoyed walking, rowing in boats and bathing, in winter sledging and figure skating. From the 19th century, the mills were gradually transformed into restaurants and the number of visitors increased. A horse-drawn bus was introduced here and in 1909, the first trolley-bus line in Bratislava. The road was made along the bottom of the valley; this is closed to transport at weekends and is used by the no. 43 bus starting from the bus stop at Patrónka. The valley begins immediately beyond the railway bridge with large car-parks. The road has a special red lane for cyclists and in-line skaters. The first reach of the valley, called Partizánska lúka (Partisan Meadow), spreads around the road with wide meadows and stream.

This area with a large number of various climbing-frames and slides, football field and places for barbecue is a genuine paradise for families with children. Two out of the valley's four ponds are near-

by. In winter, Bratislavans come here for figure skating and ice-hockey and the paths along the ponds serve as cross-country ski-trails. Directly behind the first pond stands the oldest surviving water mill from the 18th century called Klepáč (Knocker) which serves as a restaurant and a camp for young scouts. In the valley, meadows alternate with forests and ponds, and wooden shelters appear at regular intervals with barbecue pits for tourist use. Beyond the ponds, the valley broadens out and extensive meadows spread up the valley sides.

Behind the children's climbing-frames on the left, hidden in the trees, there is the chair-lift station which will take you (with your bikes) up to the top of the hill – Kamzík. This is another recreation zone for Bratislavans. In the winter, two of the slopes here are used for skiing and sledging. This is the nearest place for skiing to Bratislava. In winter, the ski-lift provides services to skiers, in summer for people using the artificial bob-sleigh run. In the neighbouring forest, high in the trees, a ropes course is constructed for people to help themselves to more adrenaline. Nearby, children can ride ponies. All around there are facilities providing snacks and drinks and the rustic-style restaurant Koliba-Expo (see p. 78) offering specialities from various parts of Slovakia. Here, you really get the impression that you are high up in the mountains. From here, you can take the chair-lift back to Železná studnička or return on foot parallel with the chair-lift along a narrow path (2.5 km). If you do not have to return, you can follow paths along the broad road leading to the 203 trolley-bus terminus. If you have time to spare, you can ascend the TV tower with its restaurant with a panoramic view of the city (p. 54).

Carpathians, Wine and Castles

The arc of the Carpathians has its beginning in Bratislava and as it curves towards the north-east it gets steadily bigger and higher. Its first part, rising right out of the city and stretching for 100 km into the distance, is called the Small Carpathian Mountains. The south-east facing slopes of the hills below the forest zone are planted with vines; at the foot of the hills, wine-producing villages and small towns were established in the Middle Ages.

📏 60-80 km

🕐🚗 Full day

ℹ️ Recommended map: VKÚ Harmanec, Malé
    Karpaty Juh, 1:25 000, č. 9

📖 Tips (See p. 131)

These villages extend like a necklace from Bratislava up to Smolenice creating the more than 60 km long Small Carpathians Wine Route. Although there are other wine-producing areas in Slovakia, the region around Bratislava is the most famous. Like pearls, massive and romantic castles and chateaux decorate the Small-Carpathian Mountains. Besides the region's eventful history, you can get familiar with the local ceramic products, taste superb wines or enjoy a local speciality – roast goose.

The Celts cultivated vines in this region more than 2,500 years ago. The vineyards flourished and were developed under the Romans and this tradition was continued by the Slavs. The first written records, however, date from as late as the 13th century when the country, devastated by the Tatars, was settled by Germans who came to cultivate the land at the invitation of the king. They introduced to this region the cultivars and culture which have survived here up to the present (see pp. 66 – 67). It may, at first glance, seem improbable today but, in the mediæval period and for a long time afterwads, Bratislava was a town of wine-growers and wine-traders. In the 16th century, the local wines were exported to many parts of Europe and the vineyards reached right up to the town's gates.

In the 19th century, Bratislava became renowned for its sparkling wine, this being the first place where it was produced outside of France (see page 66). As the town has expanded, so the vineyards have gradually diminished in their extent but even today they reach almost into the city centre.

The Small Carpathians Wine Route has its start at the eastern edge of Bratislava – in Rača – and finishes 60 kms distant in a romantic chateau in Smolenice. Beyond Rača the built-up area ends and the countryside begins. Vineyards spread over the hillsides on the left. A few kilometres further on is the small historic town of Svätý Jur (Saint George) surrounded by vineyards. In addition to its noted wine, this small town is famous for its monastery where beer is brewed. The route winds further on through vineyards past the village of Grinava. In the centre of the village a turning to the right leads to Slovenský Grob. This place has become famous for one thing only – roast goose. It is on offer all the year round but the most popular season is autumn.

Although there are quite a lot of restaurants here, it is really difficult to find an empty seat because nearly all Bratislavans come here to have some goose (see p. 81). Returning to Grinava, after just a few hundred metres at the end of the village, there is a turn to the left towards woods leading to the village of Limbach. This is probably the most beautiful village along the whole route with its well-preserved small vineyard houses. At the upper end of the village there is a restaurant famous for its specialities. The main road continues to the town of Pezinok which is the regional centre of viticulture. At the first traffic lights there is a turn towards the centre. Pezinok is a small historic town full of typical vineyard houses with long courtyards and cellars. Plenty of restaurants, small wineshops and products typical of the region are to be found here. In the upper part of the town there is a chateau dating from the 13th century famous for its spacious wine cellars. This is the home of the National Salon of Wines where you can taste and buy the best of Slovak wines. Several kms further on is the small town of Modra which is famous for its wine and also for its ceramics. Its ceramic products are available in every shop and the workshops of the main manufacturer – Majolika –are open to the public on working days.

On the hills beyond Modra stands one of the best-preserved castles in Slovakia - Červený Kameň Castle. A tour around the castle creates a big impression, due in part to its enormous wine-cellars, the most extensive in the whole of Central Europe. At weekends in the season, various festivals and historical plays are held here. The wine-route meanders through the picturesque countryside and finishes in the castle above the village of Smolenice. This gained its current appearance in the 19th century when a mediæval castle was rebuilt along the lines of a French chateau.

Trnava

The historical town of Trnava is the nearest sizeable town to Bratislava. It is proud of its great number of churches and it is one of the chief religious centres in Slovakia. Today, just as in the past, the life of this town is enriched by its university students who add to its youthful atmosphere. Trnava is rich in archaeological treasures; besides the large number of churches, the unique brick town-walls have survived the centuries as also has a complex of university buildings.

🚗 50 km

🚗🚙 Approx. 35 min on D1 motorway

🚆 Approx. 45 min departing from the Main station 🔲 1 AT 12 🖳 zsr.sk

🚌 Approx. 1 hour departing from the bus station Mlynské Nivy 🔲 1 BG 22 🖳 sad.sk

ℹ️ Tourist info: TINS, Trojičné nám. 1 🖳 trnava.sk
📞 +421 33 551 10 22 @ tins@stonline.sk

Trnava (70.000 inhabitants) is one of the oldest Slovak towns and was granted the privileges of a free royal town as early as 1238; it was founded on fertile lowland at the intersection of important trading routes and soon gained in significance, due also to the German settlers who were invited to the kingdom by King Belo IV. An extensive part of the town walls, originating from the 13th century and, uniquely in Slovakia, built of brick, has survived. There are also many surviving burghers' houses and richly-decorated religious architecture.

Following the occupation of Budín and Ostrihom by the Turks, for nearly three centuries (1541-1820) Trnava became the seat of the Ostrihom archbishop. It was the presence of the archbishop that for a long period influenced the development of the town as a centre of education. The university comprising four faculties, established by Archbishop Peter Pázmanyi flourished here in 1635

-1777. The faculties of Theology and Philosophy were opened first, then the faculty of Law and finally that of Medicine. The university comprises the largest complex of historical buildings in the town. Part of it is the first Early-Baroque building in Slovakia – the Jesuit Church of St. John the Baptist (1629-1635), also known as the university church, which was designed by Antonio Canevale and built by Pietro Spazzo.

It follows the design of Il Gesú Church in Rome. This church was the biggest and artistically the most precious building of the Counter-Reformation in Slovakia. It was decorated by Italian, Austrian and local masters. The unique three-storey wooden altar extends across the whole of the rear wall and was completed in 1640. It is one of the most beautiful churches in Slovakia, decorated with twenty-seven life-size statues. Next door to the church is the attractive building of the Rectory and opposite are two buildings of academies dating from the 18th century. The massive Gothic Church of St. Nicolas, erected at the end of the 14th century, is another valued building. After a fire, its two towers in the Gothic style were capped off with Renaissance helmets. In the 18th century, commissioned by Archbishop Imrich Eszterházi, the church was extended by a chapel designed by J. L. Hillebrandt. The elongated square next to the church which leads to the church and nunnery of the Clare nuns originating in the 13th century is lined with a row of picturesque burghers' houses.

The main square is Trinity Square, dominated by the tower in the Renaissance style dating from 1574 and the Holy Trinity Column in the Baroque style. Here are to be found the Town Hall, originally in the Renaissance style but rebuilt in the 18th century, and the first Slovak theatre dating from 1831. The streets around the square are lined with well-preserved burghers' houses with Gothic cores. With the relocation of the university to Budapest and the departure of the archbishop, the town diminished in importance for a time. However, at the turn of the 18th and 19th centuries, Trnava once more became the centre of Slovak education. In 1846, Trnava was connected with Bratislava by the first horse-drawn railway in the then Hungarian Empire which contributed substantially to the development of the town. Today, Trnava is a university town once more and one of the biggest towns in Slovakia with a rapidly expanding automobile industry due to the large Peugeot PSA production plant.

Piešťany

Less than one hour's drive from Bratislava is to be found the town which became famous for its spa. Anyone who has once experienced the hot springs and mud of Piešťany soon becomes a regular visitor. People from all over the world come here for a cure and, in increasing numbers, simply for a rest so as not to become patients in the future. For a long time now, well-being has ceased to be merely a matter of fashion, it has become a necessity. This town radiates an unusual restfulness - somehow you automatically start walking more slowly and in a more relaxed way. There are a number of beautiful parks adorned with picturesque villas and elegant hotels.

🚗 80 km

🕐🚗 Approx. 1 hour on the D1 motorway

🕐🚆 Approx. 1 h 15 min departing from the Main station 🔲 1 AT 12 ⮑ zsr.sk

🕐🚌 Approx. 1 h 30 min departing from the bus station Mlynské Nivy 🔲 1 BG 22 ⮑ sad.sk

ℹ️ Tourist info: ⮑ spa-piestany.sk
📞 +421 33 775 77 3

Between Trnava and Trenčín on the river Váh is to be found one of the most famous Slovak spa towns – Piešťany (30,000 inhabitants). The town is world-renowned for its curative hot springs with a temperature of 67-69 °C and its healing mud which together are among the best and most famous the world over. In contrast with other well-known spa towns in Slovakia, Piešťany is not located in woodland but in the lowland and has a very pleasant climate. Even the Romans were familiar with the effects of the strong and very effective hot springs and thermal mud containing hydrogen sulphide. The first written record of Piešťany dates from 1113 and the curative springs were first described in 1545. In the early stages, healing baths were prepared in holes excavated in the ground and filled with thermal water. Guests were accommodated in a very simple way in the dwellings of the local people. Only at the beginning of the 18th century, when the already famous spa became the property of the Erdödy family, were the first, originally wooden buildings, built. It was under these conditions that Ludwig van Beethoven visited the spa in 1801. At the beginning of the 19th century, several spa buildings were built, today known as the Napoleon spa, but the development was slow. In 1889, the situation changed substantially when the

spa was leased to an entrepreneur, Alexander Winter. In the course of a few years, thanks to a massive advertising campaign both at home and abroad, he managed to transform a spa of only local importance into a spa with a world-wide reputation and visited frequently by aristocrats, Indian maharajahs, Arab sheikhs and royalty. The spa experienced a major boom in visitors; new spa buildings, a sanatorium, luxury hotels and villas were constructed. In 1989, Piešťany adopted the symbol of a man breaking a crutch (the crutch-breaker). All the springs in Piešťany, especially effective in curing rheumatism and motor diseases, are located on the so-called Spa Island, washed by branches of the Váh. The water is extracted from a depth of 2000 m and the most famous spa complexes are built directly over the springs on the island. The town and the Spa Island are connected by one of the most famous features in Slovakia, with a high architectural value– the Colonnade Bridge erected in 1932 from the design of a well-known Slovak architect, Emil Belluš. The entrance to the bridge is decorated with the symbol of Piešťany, the brass statue of the crutch-breaker bearing a large inscription in Latin "Surge et ambula!" – *Arise and walk!* - to remind everybody of the reason for their visit to Piešťany. Today, as in the past, the spa is frequented by visitors from all over the world and, following an extensive reconstruction of the spa, the town's representatives are endeavouring to continue its famous history.

Trenčín

Trenčín is a prosperous, rapidly developing town which benefits from its strategic location. It is an important economic centre of Western Slovakia and is easily accessible by train or car from Bratislava. From a distance, sited on a high rock, one of the biggest castles in Slovakia will greet you. You will be enchanted by Trenčín's narrow streets and pleasant squares. In close proximity to Trenčín, in a picturesque valley, is Trenčianske Teplice, a renowned spa town, where the aristocracy used to meet in the past and which now greets clientele from all over the world.

> 🚗 120 km
>
> 🕐 🚆 1 h 15 min on the D1motorway
>
> 🕐 🚆 1 h 45 min departing from the Main Station
>   🔲 1 AT 12 ⟳ zsr.sk
>
> 🕐 🚍 2 h 15 min departing from the bus station
>   Mlynské Nivy 🔲 1 BG 22 ⟳ sad.sk
>
> ℹ️ Tourist info: Cultural and Information Centre,
>   Sládkovičova ulica ⟳ trencin.sk
>
> 📞 +421 32 7433505; fax: +421 032 743 35 05
>
> @ kic@trencin.sk

Trenčín is one of the few towns in Slovakia which can pride itself in having clear proof of its being a settlement as far back as Roman times. The material proof of a Roman legion over-wintering in the territory of the future Trenčín is engraved in the castle rock, which is the most northerly evidence located to date of a historical place where the Romans stayed in Central Europe. The inscription consists of a memorial to the victory of the emperor Marcus Aurelius over the Quadii in 179 A.D. and is accessed via the Reception of the Hotel Tatra, which was built in 1901 directly below the rock. The town only came to regional importance in the 13th century when the Castle was owned by the oligarchic Čák family. At the expense of the royal power, this family ruled over almost the whole of the territory of the then Slovakia. Although the town was, for a long time, associated with the events and history of the Castle, it began writing its own independent history when it became a free royal town with all the due privileges and duties in 1412.

Due to the strategic importance of the town, over the course of the following centuries it was the target of a number of attacks and onslaughts, all more or less successfully resisted. Trenčín to-

Trenčín

day is an important town of the Považie region (the central part of the river Váh basin) with a wonderful atmosphere. You can enjoy it on the elongated central square with a plague column dedicated to the victims of the disease which afflicted the town in 1710. The square is lined with burghers' houses and is dominated by the Early-Baroque (1653-57) church, originally Jesuit and from 1773 Piarist, and the monastery of Francis Xavier which is a unique symbiosis of architecture, sculptural art, painting and artistic stucco decoration. The *trompe l'oeil* Baroque frescoes in the interior of the church, painted by Christoph Tausch, are among the most impressive in the whole of Slovakia. The square ends with the surviving Dolná brána (Lower Gate) of the town fortifications dating from the 15th century. Beyond the Gate is another pleasant square with cafés and restaurants and a popular fountain with a statue of a water sprite in the centre. An integral part of the town panorama is the neighbouring massive building of a synagogue with a cupola built in the Art-Nouveau style in 1912. Today, it serves as a room for occasional exhibitions and in its rear part there is a prayer room. The town and the Castle are connected by means of a covered stairway dating from 1568 which provided a rapid communication route for defenders hurrying to the fortification walls via the church of the Birth of the Virgin Mary from the 14th century.

The church, along with the noted two-storey charnel house of St. Michael in the Gothic style from the 15th century and the parish church, form a fortified complex situated on a plateau above the square, known as Marienberg. The tiny street leading down into the town is dominated by the very interesting Executioner's House from the 17th century.

One of the biggest castles in Slovakia was constructed as a frontier castle on the Western border of "Upper Hungary" guarding the valley of the Váh. A stone castle with a massive watchtower stood here as early as the 11th century. This was replaced by the Roman Great Tower in the 13th century. The basis of the Castle is formed by four palaces in the Gothic style from the 14th and the 15th centuries: Matúšov (Matthew's), Ľudovítov (Louis's), Barborin (Barbora's) and Zápoľskovcov (the Zápoľský family). They were combined in an ingenious system of fortresses which was extended in the Renaissance period by a star-shaped anti-artillery bastion designed by Italian builders. Due to this, the Castle was not conquered in the Turkish assaults in 1663.

Hammam

The Castle was the seat of one of the most important oligarchs in the country at the beginning of the 14th century – Matúš Čák – who, at the expense of the royal power, appropriated two thirds of the territory of present-day Slovakia. The castle tower is 30 m high and affords a spectacular view over the valley of the Váh and the surrounding wooded hills.

Close to Trenčín, one of the most famous spas in Slovakia – Trenčianske Teplice – is set in picturesque countryside. The thermal springs (37-40°C) and mud are used in healing motor and nervous system disorders. For centuries, the springs belonged to the owners of Trenčín Castle. The oldest record in writing of the existence of the mineral springs dates from 1398. In 1580, the spa is mentioned in historical documents; the number of spa houses steadily increased. From the beginning of the 17th century up to 1835, the spa was owned by the Illésházy dynasty, which tried to adopt a similar style in constructing it as was usual in other renowned spa towns in the monarchy.

However, in this respect, success only came when the spa was purchased by a Viennese banker, Georg Sina and his successors. In the course of building activities in 1870, the well-known spa house "Sina" was constructed and in 1888, Georg Sina's granddaughter – Iphigenie d'Harcourt – commissioned probably the best-known oriental-style spa house "Hammam". Thanks to this dynasty, Trenčianske Teplice acquired its reputation for excellence at the end of the 19th century. In the decades that followed, a large number of buildings were erected which added to the picture built up by this pleasant little spa town which today is trying to return to its famous past.

Trenčianske Teplice

Nitra

Nitra (87,000 inhabitants) is a town with a very rich and moving history and today it is one of the biggest of Slovak towns. It was from this point that Christianity spread across the country and today Nitra is still the seat of a cardinal. It is a centre of the south-western part of the country with highly developed industry and, thanks to its two universities, a lively student atmosphere. You can extend your walk through the pleasant old town with an attractive pedestrian zone up to the Castle which dominates the surrounding countryside and also offers a spectacular view of the town.

🚗 90 km

🕐🚗 Approx. 50 min on the D1 motorway and then R1

🕐🚆 Approx. 2 h departing from the Main station 🔲 1 AT 12 ➔ zsr.sk

🕐🚌 Approx. 1 h 30 min departing from the bus station Mlynské Nivy 🔲 1 BG 22 ➔ sad.sk

ℹ️ Tourist info: NISYS, Štefánikova 1
➔ nisys.sk ➔ nitra.sk
📞 +421 037 16186; +421 037 7410906; fax: +421 037 7410907 @ info@nitra.sk

The symbol of Nitra, the oldest Slovak town, is the prominent castle hill below which the Nitra river runs, with the typical silhouette of its tower. As early as 828, Count Pribina, the then ruler of the Nitra principality, commissioned the first Christian church on the

territory occupied by Slavs and invited Adalram, Archbishop of Salzburg, to consecrate it. From 880 onwards, the town was the seat of the bishopric and over the following centuries Nitra became established as an important cultural centre. In 1248, it was granted the privileges of a free royal town. The historical part of today's Nitra comprises the Castle and the Upper and Lower Town. Nitra Castle is one of the most interesting castle complexes in the whole of Slovakia and includes the Castle Cathedral, Bishop's Palace and fortification. The Cathedral of St. Emeram, made up of three interconnected churches, is the most noteworthy part. The Roman church dating from the 11th century, today in ruins, is the oldest. The Gothic style Upper church from 1333-1335, whose interior has twice been reconstructed, stands a little higher. In the 17th and the 18th centuries it was richly decorated with frescoes and paintings by Antonio Galliarti. As the main part of the Cathedral, it is one of the most prized sacred interiors in the Baroque style in Slovakia. It is connected with the most recent

Lower Church by a wide flight of steps. This was constructed in the Baroque style in 1622-1642 and complements the whole Baroque complex. The Bishop's Palace with courtyard erected in 1732-39 on the site of an older palace in the Gothic style stands next to the Cathedral. The star-shaped fortification of the castle complex was completed in 1674 in response to the defeat and destruction of the town by the Turks in 1663. Below the Castle, the Upper Town is dominated by the attractive small square with the building of the Great Seminary from the 18th century with the much-prized Diocesan Library. Opposite stands the building of the Small Seminary, dating from the 19th century. Kluch Palace from the beginning of the 19th

century is an interesting building with a large figure of a telamon on the corner whose popular name *Corgoň* is used as the brand-name for the beer produced in the Nitra brewery. The Lower Town with its pleasant pedestrian zone leading into the spacious square

with a modern theatre and the Town Hall dating from 1880 is the vital centre of Nitra. The recently restored synagogue from 1911 serves as an exhibition hall. One of the dominant features of the town is the massive Piarist church and monastery in the Baroque style dating from 1701-1763 decorated with valuable Late Baroque wall paintings. Beyond the river, the extensive hill of Zobor towers over the town; since it rises from the lowlands of southern Slovakia it is a conspicuous prominence, visible in good weather conditions even from Bratislava. The Zobor hillsides conceal the remnants of the Benedictine monastery which was founded before 1000 and fell into disuse in the 15th century. The monks of this monastery, the oldest in the territory of present day Slovakia, left the so-called Zobor records describing the monastery and the surrounding area. These documents, dating from 1111-1113, are the oldest surviving written records in the territory of Slovakia. It is also thanks to the monks that Nitra has a rich tradition of viticulture.

Komárno

A brief glance reveals that the south of Slovakia is a special part of the country. It has the warmest climate and the most fertile land, suited to growing fruit and vegetables; on the other hand, it is the least forested and the lowest-lying part of Slovakia. It is rich in natural thermal springs which are popular recreation resorts for locals and visitors alike. In the past, Komárno (38,000 inhabitants), as one of the centres of this region, was the largest stronghold in Central Europe and, thanks to its rich history, it is still attractive. This part of the country is inhabited by the Hungarian minority and both languages are in use. Although a relatively small area, the southern part of the country contributes to the diversity of Slovakia.

- 100 km
- cca. 1h 30 min on road No. 63
- cca. 2 h departing from the main railway station 🔍 1 AT 12 ⮂ zsr.sk
- cca. 2 h 15 min departing from the bus station Mlynské Nivy 🔍 1 BG 22 ⮂ sad.sk
- Župná ulica (street) 5 ⮂ infokomarno.sk
- +421 035 7730 063 @ tik@infokomarno.sk

From ancient times, due to its strategic position at the confluence of two major rivers – the Danube and the Váh - Komárno has been a crossroads of several important trade routes and a focus of interest for the powerful. It is not surprising then that the town was built as a stronghold which resisted the attacks of the Tatars in 1242. The Danube divides the town into two parts; the part in Hungary is called Komárom. The proximity of the border and the mix of inhabitants give Komárno its special and pleasant atmosphere. It is one of centres of the Hungarian minority in Slovakia and the seat of the University for the Hungarian minority.

At the time of the Turkish incursion in the 16th and 17th centuries, Komárno was transformed at great cost into one of the most important anti-Turkish forts in the empire, making use of all the latest technological achievements. The stronghold consists of three parts. The Old Fort dates from the 12th century and the building work was finished in the 16th century. The New Fort with its pentagonal plan was constructed in 1663-1673 and subsequently connected to the old part. The most recent part is formed by a ring of fortification walls and bastions, known as the Palatine Line, and was built during the Napoleonic wars in the 19th century.

The impregnable stronghold in Komárno is the largest in Central Europe and is gradually being made accessible to the public. At the end of the 18th century, Komárno experienced a series of earthquakes which seriously affected the life of the town. Due to the extensive damage, for a long time the law did not permit the construction of buildings of more than two storeys.

Besides the stronghold and the historical part with its pleasant streets and squares, the Square of Europe, which was built in an empty area in the centre of the town, has become one of the town's current attractions. At the former crossroads of ancient trade routes of European significance, the square was created and symbolically lined with buildings having the typical architectural features of forty-five different European countries. There is also the Millennium Fountain, shops, cafés and many benches from which you can inspect the individual buildings. A stroll around the town leads you past the birth-places of two famous artists. The Hungarian writer Mór Jókai and the well-known music composer Franz Lehár were both born in Komárno. After Bratislava, Komárno is the second largest inland port in Slovakia and the local shipyards are renowned for the construction of river and ocean-going ships. At Patince, close to Komárno, there is a popular recreation resort with thermal springs.

- ⮂ wellness.sk
- ⮂ termalsro.sk

Map

Tips

Svätý Jur: vinnepivnice.sk

Slovenský Grob: grobskydvor.sk
zlatahus.sk stolcekprestrisa.sk

Limbach: hotellimbach.sk

Pezinok: restauraciamatysak.sk
National Wine Salon nsvsr.sk

Modra:
urichtara.com majolika.sk elesko.sk

Červený Kameň:
hradcervenykamen.sk

Smolenice: kcsmolenice.sav.sk
vintour.sk

Essentials

Arrival

1 Before Leaving

Although Slovakia is right in the centre of Europe, it is only recently that it has become known as a tourist destination. Due to this, many people feel a lack of information about this beautiful country which has so much to offer. The following official pages provide you with complete information about Bratislava and Slovakia:

| 🌐 visit.bratislava.sk | 🌐 cometoslovakia.com |
| 🌐 slovakiatourism.sk | |

2 Information

In some countries, Slovakia has opened offices affiliated to the Slovak Tourist Board whose employees are ready to help you. Current information as to where these representatives are situated in European capitals is available at:

| 🌐 slovakiatourism.sk |

3 Bratislava Airport (BTS)

Bratislava airport can be reached from the city centre in 15 – 20 minutes. There are direct flights to a number of destinations in Europe and a number of low-cost carriers operate here. A taxi to the city centre costs around EUR 15. You can save some money if you take the no. 61 bus to the main train station. From here it takes about 15 minutes to get to the city centre on foot or 2-3 bus stops by bus no. 93. Bus tickets are available from ticket-machines at bus-stops or in kiosks. They must be validated in the buses.

| 🌐 airportbratislava.sk | 🌐 skyeurope.com |

4 Vienna-Schwechat (VIE) Airport

The airport at Vienna-Schwechat is only about 40 km west of Bratislava and Slovaks mainly use it for long-haul flights. In effect, it is one of the gateways to Slovakia. Buses to Bratislava depart at 30 to 60 minute intervals. Tickets may be bought on the bus.

| 🌐 viennaairport.com | 🌐 blaguss.at |
| 🌐 eurolines.sk | |

5 Train

There are main lines from Prague, Budapest, Vienna and elsewhere in Slovakia. Bratislava has two railway stations – the Main Station (🔲 1 AT 12) and Petržalka (🔲 3 FF 12). The Main Station is very well connected with all of the city via trams, buses or trolleybuses. You can get to the Old Town on foot in only 15 min-

utes. From the train station in Petržalka, the no. 80, 91, 93 buses take you to the city centre.

| 🌐 zrs.sk |

6 Bus

Bratislava is also conveniently connected with many European cities via a network of bus lines. It has frequent services to its close surrounding areas and also to other regions in Slovakia. Buses arrive and depart from Mlynské Nivy bus station (🔲 1 BG 22). Coaches between Bratislava and Vienna run at one-hour intervals.

| 🌐 eurolines.sk | 🌐 studentagency.sk |
| 🌐 blaguss.at | |

7 Boat

Due to its position on the Danube, Bratislava has regular connections by boat with Vienna and Budapest. The centre of Vienna (Schwedenplatz) is connected with Bratislava by a fast catamaran Twin City Liner and another fast hydrofoil which is berthed at Vienna Handelskai. This one also goes to Budapest.

| 🌐 twincityliner.com | 🌐 lod.sk |

8 Car

Bratislava is situated at the intersection of several important motorways. Distance to Prague is 330 km, Budapest 200 km and Vienna 65 km. On motorways, a car must display a motorway sticker, available at borders or filling stations. The minimum period of validity of a sticker is one week.

9 Crossing the Border

Since 2004, Slovakia has been a member of the EU. Visitors to Slovakia travelling from other EU countries, Switzerland, Liechtenstein, Norway and Iceland only need to have a valid ID card. In 2007, Slovakia became part of the Schengen group of countries without border controls. A list of the countries whose citizens are required to have a visa can be found at:

| 🌐 foreign.gov.sk |

10 Permitted Goods

There is no requirement to declare the following quantities of tobacco products: 400 pcs of cigarettes or 200 pcs of cigars or 400 pcs cigarillos or 1 kg of smoking tobacco or their proportional combination. Where alcohol is concerned: 10 l spirits or 90 l wine or 110 l beer or 20 l of aperitifs or their proportional combination.

Local Transport

1 Trams

Trams are the most significant form of public transport in the city. They are reliable and on time. They also are the fastest public means of transport. In general, they start at 5 a.m. and finish at 11:30 p.m. Tickets are valid for a certain period of time and are available from ticket-machines or kiosks. They must be validated once inside the tram. They are valid for all means of public transport in the city and remain valid when changing from one means of transport to another. Tickets have a minimum period of validity of 15 minutes and the longest is 7 days.

📄 imhd.sk

2 Buses

As well as trams, buses also play a substantial role in the public transport system. Limited-stop services run on the longer routes through the city. After midnight, night buses operate in Bratislava at roughly one hour intervals.

3 Trolley-Buses

Some routes in the city centre, mainly in its hilly parts, are electrified and serviced by trolley-buses. They have a long tradition in Bratislava and have been operating here for more than 100 years.

4 Bratislava City Card

If you plan to stay in the city for one, two or three days, there is nothing quite as practical and advantageous as the City Card. It entitles you to free of charge urban transport and a guided tour in the Old Town and 10-20% reduction in admission fees to museums, galleries, trips as well as taxi and car-hire. The card is available from all the BKIS enquiry centres (p. 136).

📄 bkis.sk   📄 visit.bratislava.sk

5 Boats

Excursion boats run on the Danube in Bratislava from April to October. They depart from the passenger port on the Danube bank (🔲 2 DB 31). From the boat you can see how dynamically the city is developing and the role the Danube plays in it. A round trip takes about 45 minutes, the trip to Devín Castle 1 ½ hours.

📄 lod.sk

6 Car

Driving in the city has become more and more difficult. Although there has been an increase in the number of motorways and bridges, there has also been an increase in the number of cars. The worst periods are between 8:00 and 9:00 and 16:30 to 17:30. The speed limit in the city is 50 km per hour unless indicated otherwise.

7 Parking

The main roads in the city are provided with digital information displays showing the current number of vacant places in underground garages or in car parks. Street-parking in the city centre is a paid service. You are required to use a scratch-card available from agents wearing yellow waistcoats or in kiosks.

8 Taxi

Despite the rumours, taxi drivers in Bratislava are reliable and fair. They are mostly local people who are familiar with every single street. Bratislava is not a large city so probably the longest route you take will be to the airport which costs approx. EUR 15.

ℹ️ Profi Taxi 📞 02 16222, ABC Taxi 📞 02 16100

9 Bicycle

The local people are great cycling enthusiasts but mostly as a sort of sport or an active relaxation (pp. 121, 122, 123). It is rare to see people riding bikes to work as is quite usual in other European cities. Cycle-paths generally run along the Danube or in the suburban areas of the city and they are not yet inter-connected.

📄 cyklotrasy.sk

10 On Foot

A great advantage of Bratislava is the compactness of its centre. In addition, the whole of the Old Town is an extensive pedestrian zone. The Old Town and the Castle are readily connected so most of the attractions for which visitors come to Bratislava can be accessed on foot.

Tourist Info

1 BKIS

The main tourist information centre has its office in the Old Town on Klobučnícka street (⬛ 2 CX 22). Here, the staff will advise you on accommodation, attractions, cultural events, transport etc. Internet is also available in this centre. Smaller subsidiary offices are also to be found at the airport, the main train station (⬛ 1 AT 12) and the passenger port (⬛ 2 DB 31), ☎ 00421 2 16186.

| ⇨ bkis.sk | ⇨ visit.bratislava.sk |

2 Newspapers

If you want to learn more about events in Slovakia, journals and magazines written in English and German are also printed here. The best-known is The Slovak Spectator weekly, www.thedaily.sk, Spectacular Slovakia, Business Journal Slovakia or Pressburger Zeitung. The best selection of foreign press is available at the Interpress shops (⬛ 2 CU 28, 2 CR 23).

| ⇨ slovakspectator.sk | ⇨ thedaily.sk |

3 Shopping

In recent years, the way of shopping in Bratislava has changed considerably. You can shop either in the cosy Old Town where opening hours in shops are usually from 10 a.m. to 6 p.m. and to 1 p.m. on Saturdays or in a number of large shopping centres on the outskirts of the city. The opening hours in these centres are from 10 (9) a.m. to 9 (10) p.m. daily. There are three Tesco hypermarkets in Bratislava open 24 hours a day (pp. 102-103)

4 National Holidays

Slovakia is a country with one of the greatest number of national holidays in Europe – 15 in total. These are: 1st January, 6th January, Good Friday, Easter Monday, 1st May, 8th May, 5th July, 29th August, 1st September, 15th September, 1st November, 17th November, 24th December, 25th December and 26th December. On these days, usually only the shopping centres and hypermarkets are open.

5 Money

The currency in Slovakia has been the Euro since 1st. January 2009. Most shops accept international bank cards. If, however, you want to exchange currency anyway, you can do so in banks, exchange offices or in a large number of ATMs.

6 Internet

If you are not staying in a hotel with a room provided with internet, there are other ways to get connected with the world. Hot spots are to be found on Primaciálne (Primate's Sq., ⬛ 2 CV 22) Squares. Internet access is also available at the BKIS (top of page). In the Old Town, there are several internet cafés:

| ℹ Klarinet, Klariská 4 (⬛ 2 CQ 22), open Mon – Fri 10 a.m. - 10 p.m, Sat, Sun 3 p.m. – 10 p.m. |

7 Weather

Bratislava has a temperate continental climate with warm summers and cold winters. The average daily temperature in summer (July, August) reaches 21 °C (maximum 38 °C), the average daily temperature in winter (December, January) –1 °C (minimum – 20 °C). The months with the highest rainfall are July and September; on the other hand May and October are relatively dry. The best times to visit Bratislava are from mid-April to mid-October and just before Christmas.

8 Regular City Tours

There are several ways to get familiar with the city. You can choose from different routes. Another attraction is a tour around the Old Town in a replica of a small historic carriage called Prešporáčik. For anyone who wants to see the Old Town under his or her own steam, the services of the BKIS (⬛ 2 CX 22) might be useful.

| ⇨ presporacik.sk | ⇨ bkis.sk |

9 Mail and Telephones

Postage stamps are available at post offices and also from kiosks. The Main Post Office is conveniently situated in the Old Town on SNP Square 34-35 (⬛ 2 CU 19). The office is open Mon-Fri 7 a.m. – 8 p.m, Sat 7 a.m. – 6 p.m, Sun 9 a.m. – 2 p.m. Following the invasion of cellular phones, there are only a few telephone boxes operational in the city, mostly using a phonecard. International cards are available from kiosks and at post offices. The country code for Slovakia is 00421, Bratislava 02 (just 2 if calling from abroad); local telephone numbers have 8 digits.s.

10 Car-Hire

Bratislava has branches of some international car-hire firms such as Hertz, Avis, Sixt, Europcar, etc. They have offices in the big hotels and at the airport. However, there are local car-hire firms offering comparable quality at cheaper rates.

| ⇨ abrix.sk | ⇨ autodanubius.sk |

Health and Security

1 Emergency Telephone Numbers:

112	Emergency calls
158	Police
150	Fire Service
159	City Police
18 124	Vehicle clamping and removal service

2 Hospitals

In the event of you needing medical treatment, look for it in one of the four following big faculty hospitals. Most of the doctors speak English. As tourists are largely concentrated in the Old Town, you will probably try the first one:
the Old Town – Mickiewiczova st.13 (🔍 2 DH 8);
Kramáre – Limbová st.5 (🔍 1 AJ 4);
Ružinov – Ružinovská st.6 (🔍 3 FL 6);
Petržalka – Antolská st.11 (🔍 3 FF 14).

☞ faneba.sk

3 Private Clinics

If you plan to stay in Bratislava for a longer period or you come to live here, it is advisable to find a private medical office providing greater comfort and facilities. The following are some reputable private clinics: Pro sanus, Medifera, Medical Care, Hippokrates, Sport Clinic, Sanatorium Koch, Schill Dental.

☞ medicalcare.sk	☞ medifera.sk
☞ sportclinic.sk	☞ sanatoriumkoch.sk
☞ schill.sk	☞ prosanus.sk
☞ hippokrates.sk	

4 Health Insurance

In the EU and EEA member states, it is possible to obtain an EHIC card which entitles you to medical care at a reduced price or even free of charge in a public health office of another member state under the same conditions as the local insurees. This is recommended as supplementary to a private insurance.

5 Pharmacies

Pharmacies are identified by a green cross. They are plentiful and usually open from 7 a.m. to 6 p.m. and on Saturday to 1 p.m. The only pharmacy providing a 24-hour emergency service is situated at the eastern part of the Old Town: Lekáreň pod Manderlom, Nám. SNP 20, 🔍 2 DA 22.

6 Pickpockets

Like all larger cities, Bratislava also has a problem with pickpockets. They operate in crowded places, hence they are found in the popular Old Town and on public transport. As a result of the introduction of cameras, the situation has improved considerably but the thieves are very inventive. Most thefts are committed in crowds of people or in shops. It is advisable to carry your bags in front of you.

7 Crime Rate

In comparison with other big cities, the crime rate here is relatively low. Bratislava does not have anywhere that could be termed as a dangerous quarter. The city centre popular with tourists is well-lit even at night and is monitored by a camera system. However, this does not mean that one does not have to be watchful especially in deserted and dark places. Tourists should carry their ID (EU) or passport with them at all times.

8 Women on Their Own

Bratislava is a modern city with a relatively young population so a woman on her own is nothing unusual. In general, men are attentive towards women; however, their attitude depends on their generation and education. As is true in other big cities, it is not sensible for women to be out on their own in provocative clothes in the night in dark places.

9 Cars

Shortly after the fall of communism, Bratislava gained a reputation as a city where it was inadvisable to have an expensive car with foreign number-plates. Since then, however, the situation has changed radically and although car theft has not been totally eradicated, the situation in Bratislava is incomparably better than in other neighbouring cities. It is important not to provoke theft by leaving a handbag or notebook on view.

10 Embassies

Most of the embassies of countries important to Slovakia have their residences in the Old Town and in the villa quarters below and above the Castle. Some states have their embassies to Slovakia in Vienna, Prague or Budapest. On the maps on the inside cover of this guide, flags are depicted to symbolise embassies. A current list of embassies and contact numbers can be found at:

 ☞ mfa.sk

Useful Things to Know

1 A Visit

If you get an invitation to visit someone's home, do not be surprised to find that your hosts expect you to take your shoes off. Sometimes you will even be offered slippers. It is probable that your hosts will try to persuade you to keep your shoes on but you will show respect for the tradition if you do take them off. It is usual to take some flowers for the hostess and a bottle of wine or other alcoholic beverage for the host. Slovaks enjoy eating so you can expect to be offered food during your visit.

2 Drinking and Driving

Slovakia is a country where there is always an opportunity to drink. Locals will offer you alcohol even if they are aware that you came by car. Nevertheless, there is zero tolerance for alcohol being found in a driver's bloodstream. Checks are frequent and the penalties severe. If you want to enjoy your time, you had better take a taxi or drink something non-alcoholic.

3 Tips

Tips are usually rounded up; with higher expenses there is a rule of a 10 % tip but the actual tip depends on your satisfaction. In ordinary restaurants the waiter will usually bring your bill, tell you the sum and wait until you pay. As a rule, the total sum including a tip is paid or you indicate by a gesture that they may keep the change.

4 Czechs, Slovenians

Slovaks are a small nation but proud of their identity and language. Only few foreigners are aware that the former Czechoslovakia was a federation of two republics – Czech and Slovak – and that, historically, two official languages always existed side by side: the Czech and the Slovak languages. And also that Czechs and Slovaks are two separate nations, despite being close. To confuse Czechs and Slovaks would not be a polite gesture. The same is true for Slovenia. It has a similar name and national flag but it is a totally different country.

5 Give up a Seat

If you use one of the forms of urban transport and it is crowded, young people, especially young men, usually give up their seats to older people, especially women, women with children and pregnant women. If you do not do so, some-body may tell you to do so which, if it happens, is not at all pleasant.

6 Good Manners

If you want to try to speak Slovak, be aware that a substantial difference exists between addressing somebody who is not familiar to you and your friend. Just as in French, so in Slovak also, the second person plural is used in this case. Also address this person by his/her surname and use different greetings than you would with your friends (p. 139).

7 Even Number of Flowers

If you buy a bunch of flowers for a living person, make sure that you only give them an odd number of flowers (in cases where the flowers are readily countable). An even number of flowers is reserved for the dead. It is an old custom dating back to the period of the Austro-Hungarian Empire and the same applies in the neighbouring countries.

8 Inappropriate Clothes

In general, people in Bratislava dress smartly, another custom dating from the time of the Empire which it has in common with Vienna. Bratislava has a long musical tradition and to go to the opera or to the philharmony in sweater and jeans would be considered impolite, although people would not express their disapproval.

9 Black Passengers

In comparison with other cities, black passengers on the various forms of urban transport are treated quite severely in Bratislava. Checks are frequent and the inspectors are always in plain clothes. In order to avoid an unpleasant situation, remember that the ticket you bought from a ticket-machine at a bus-stop or from a kiosk must be validated on board. Tickets are not sold on board the urban transport.

10 Coffee

Just like Vienna, Bratislava is famous for its café culture. There are a number of different ways of making coffee so to simply ask for a coffee will bring a smile to the face of the person serving you. He or she will immediately offer you at least ten possible choices..

Phrasebook

á, é, í, ó, ú	acute accent (it lengthens the vowel sound, like: father, air, knee, door, moon)
ď, ť, ň, ľ	a diacritical mark which softens the consonant, as in: duty, tube, canyon, lute
ô	like quotation
ä	similar to ae

1 Language

Slovak is one of the western Slavonic languages like Czech and Polish. These languages are fairly similar and the ones that Slovaks understand best. However, this does not mean that they do not understand other Slavonic languages such as Croatian and Russian. It's as if Slovak were a kind of Esperanto of the Slavonic languages as a result of its geographical position in the centre and the fact that the difference between Slovak and the neighbouring language is never very big. Although there are only just over five million Slovak speakers, the speakers of this language are able to understand more than 300 million people.

2 Grammar

Slovak grammar poses the greatest problem for foreigners. To a large extent it is influenced by Latin so be prepared for declensions, grammatical cases, genders etc. At least you can console yourself with the fact that Slovaks themselves have problems with it, also. School children often find it difficult to distinguish between the usage of "i" and "y", especially when there is no difference in pronunciation. There is no other way – you just have to learn by heart the so-called selected words in which "y" is used.

3 Pronunciation

The pronunciation might seem to be quite complicated; however, once you learn the rules, it is quite simple. In Slovak, the general rule "write as you hear it" is valid so there is one letter to every sound. The letter "ch" is the exception to the rule which exists as an independent letter in Slovak alphabet. It is not like English where one letter can be pronounced in a number of different ways nor is there the need for three letters to produce one sound as in German. The pronunciation of vowels and some consonants is similar to Italian or Spanish. It is useful to remember that, unlike most other Slavonic languages, the stress is placed on the initial syllable.

c	oats
č	like cheese
š	like shampoo
ž	like aubergine
j	like yes
g	like goal
ch	like loch in Scottish
dž	like jazz
r	as in Scottish

4 Numbers

1	jeden
2	dva
3	tri
4	štyri
5	päť
6	šesť
7	sedem
8	osem
9	deväť
10	desať
11	jedenásť
20	dvadsať
21	dvadsať jeden
100	sto
500	päťsto
1000	tisíc

5 Vocabulary and Phrases

Good afternoon	Dobrý deň
Good morning	Dobré ráno
Good evening	Dobrý večer
Hi / Hello	Ahoj / servus
Good bye	Dovidenia
Thank you	Ďakujem
Please	Prosím
Please here you are	Nech sa páči
Excuse me / Sorry	Prepáčte / Pardón
Yes / No	Áno / nie
How much is it?	Koľko to stojí?
Where is…?	Kde je…?
Good / Bad	Dobre / zle
Yesterday / Today / Tomorrow	Včera / dnes / zajtra
Right / Left / Straight	Vpravo / vľavo / rovno
My name is …	Volám sa…
I understand / I don't understand	Rozumiem / nerozumiem
Mr / Mrs/ Miss	Pán / pani / slečna
Monday / Tuesday / Wednesday / Thursday / Friday / Saturday / Sunday	Pondelok / utorok / streda / štvrtok / piatok / sobota / nedeľa
Day / Week / Year	Deň / týždeň / rok

Index

General Index

Street Index

MAP 2

LOCAL CUISINE AT ITS BEST

Gorkého 5, Bratislava | www.beerpalace.sk

Unique concept combining tasty local food, fresh beer and great ambiance with live music in the premises of a historic palace.

Michalská 4, Bratislava | www.presburgrestaurant.s

Recalling times when Bratislava was known as Pressburg, this restaurant is bringing grandma's specialities served in the traditional way in historic ambiance.

Hviezdoslavovo nám. 20, Bratislava | www.carnevalle

Carnevalle is bringing top quality ingredients combined in regional and international cuisine to offer fine dining for (not only) meat lovers. Nice to meat you!

Hviezdoslavovo nám. 19, Bratislava | www.zylinder

Once Bratislava (Pressburg) was at the heart of the Habsburg monarchy. Zylinder is bringing back the best of traditional regional recepies with a modern touch at one of the town's best addresses.

LOOK FOR LOGOS ON THE MAP